Lorraine Richardson is an experienced property solicitor and trainer who is a popular conference and CPD speaker. Lorraine is now freelance but when in practice she ran a branch office and was a partner and the COLP for her firm.

She also designs and delivers property and legal skills related courses and online materials including Conveyancing Quality Scheme training for the Law Society.

Lorraine has developed a skill for writing and delivering webinars and aims to produce work that is both interesting and accessible for the viewer. Lorraine is the major writer for the monthly update journal for practitioners, the 'Practical Lawyer.'

Lorraine has set up her own company, Adapt Law Limited, and offers property related courses and webinars and a membership scheme for firms to access her webinars and personalised conveyancing training.

For more information go to www.adaptlaw.co.uk

A Practical Guide to Document Signing and Electronic Signatures for Conveyancers

Second Edition

A Practical Guide to Document Signing and Electronic Signatures for Conveyancers

Second Edition

Lorraine Richardson

M.A. (Cantab)

Law Brief Publishing

Published 2022 by Law Brief Publishing, an imprint of Law Brief Publishing Ltd
30 The Parks
Minehead
Somerset
TA24 8BT

www.lawbriefpublishing.com

Paperback: 978-1-914608-57-5

For Gabriella

PREFACE TO THE FIRST EDITION

The irony of me writing a guide which encompasses electronic signatures will not be lost on anyone who knows me. I'm not known for my IT skills which largely extend only to applying bold and italic styles. But this is precisely why I have written this guide. I am a conveyancer of a certain age who has spent her entire career doing conveyancing based on the traditional form of signatures, namely asking the client to sign their name with a pen.

The challenges of Covid-19, the almost overnight move to homeworking for many conveyancers and the inability to meet our clients face to face has led to a very swift move towards the use of electronic signatures in conveyancing becoming mainstream.

What I am seeking to do in this Practical Guide is to broadly outline where we are in terms of the law on signing contracts and deeds and to suggest to conveyancers steps that they might take to help them effectively embrace new ways of working, should they choose to adopt them.

Conveyancing is fraught with risk, and in my opinion adopting electronic signatures presents a new series of risks for conveyancers to grapple with. I have tried to take a neutral stance on whether witnessed electronic signatures are a good thing – some firms have already embraced them; others will never want to deal with them. I am naturally risk averse which is why I have highlighted risks which conveyancers should be considering, but I have not sought to reach a conclusion on the issue of risk because this is an assessment which each firm must make.

I hope that some of the pointers and questions will help conveyancers to frame their thinking when deciding whether to adopt electronic signatures and, if so, to help them choose an appropriate provider. My pointers are the starting point for conveyancers when thinking about these issues, but I do not hold these out as being the only questions to ask!

My heartfelt thanks go to Tim and Garry at Law Brief Publishing for giving me the opportunity to write this book; it is the first in the 'Conveyancing Companion' series. I also thank those close to me for putting up with the constant refrain of 'I'm working'. And special thanks to my lovely friend Prof Peter Lyons from CPD Training (UK) Limited who has telephoned me without fail every week since I became freelance to inspire and encourage me.

The law described in this book is up to date as at 15 March 2021.

Lorraine Richardson
March 2021

PREFACE TO THE SECOND EDITION

There are few areas where the law is more fast moving than in the area of digital identity and electronic signing of documents. Add a pandemic and unprecedented work levels into the mix and property lawyers have got a lot to think about.

I wrote the first edition on 'A Practical Guide to Document Signing and Electronic Signatures for Conveyancers' (2021) in response to HMLR's confirmation during the depths of the pandemic in 2020 that it would accept deeds for registration signed using Mercury signatures and witnessed electronic signatures. All of this information was included in Practice Guide 8. At HMLR's invitation, I made some comments on PG 8 at the time to which they kindly responded:

> *'I am grateful for Lorraine's very substantial help when we were developing our practice regarding electronic signatures and Practice Guide 8. She made many suggestions as to how we might improve the Practice Guide and provided possible wording: we adopted most of Lorraine's suggestions and much of her wording.'*
>
> ***Emily d'Albuquerque,***
> ***Deputy Director, Central Legal Services,***
> ***HM Land Registry***

Just over 12 months from publication, HMLR has consolidated its requirements on electronic signatures of deeds into a new Practice Guide 82 and has removed the content from PG8. HMLR has replaced the term 'witnessed electronic signatures' with the more accurate term 'conveyancer-certified electronic signatures'. This updated version of the book incorporates these changes and reference to further guidance and resources that have been introduced by various organisations in the 12 months since publication. In addition, there is a new section on whether conveyancers should accept contracts signed electronically, if this has not been agreed between the conveyancers prior to exchange of contracts.

However, its heart, the purpose of this book remains as per the original: to help conveyancers who are considering investing in a product that incorporates the facility for documents to be signed electronically to ask the right questions. There is a dizzying array of providers and products and not all of them incorporate HMLR's very specific requirements. Conveyancers need to think about cost, security, longevity, existing systems and risk and I hope to help conveyancers gather their thoughts to help them avoid making an expensive mistake.

The law is believed to be correct and up to date as at 25 June 2022.

Lorraine Richardson
June 2022

LEGAL NOTICE

Conveyancing is by its nature a risky business. Throughout this Practical Guide suggestions to assist conveyancers in managing some of these risks are made. However, risk cannot be eliminated, it can only be mitigated. It is the responsibility of those in practice to ensure that they comply with their legal and regulatory obligations. We are not attempting to cover every technical nuance and argument which might be presented in court if the validity of a signed document is challenged. This Practical Guide discusses day-to-day challenges and issues for conveyancers and endeavours to provide suggestions to assist.

We have made every effort to ensure that the content of this Practical Guide is accurate. However, any outcomes or recommendations are just our opinion as to what steps you might wish to take in practice. The contents of this Practical Guide do not constitute legal advice and must not be relied upon as advice.

ABBREVIATIONS

2006 Act – Companies Act 2006

Cilex – Chartered Institute of Legal Executives

CLC – Council for Licensed Conveyancers

CQS – Conveyancing Quality Scheme

FCA – Financial Conduct Authority

HMLR – Her Majesty's Land Registry

HMRC – Her Majesty's Revenue & Customs

ICO – Information Commissioner's Office

LPA 1925 – Law of Property Act 1925

LRA 2002 – Land Registration Act 2002

LRR 2003 – Land Registration Rules 2003

Protocol – Law Society Conveyancing Protocol

1989 Act – Law of Property (Miscellaneous Provisions) Act 1989

SRA – Solicitors Regulation Authority

UK Finance Handbook – UK Finance Mortgage Lender's Handbook for Conveyancers

CONTENTS

Preface to the First Edition

Preface to the Second Edition

Legal Notice

Abbreviations

Introduction		1
Chapter One	What Is a Signature?	3
Chapter Two	The Contract and Deeds in Conveyancing	13
Chapter Three	HMLR Acceptance of Electronic Signatures on Deeds – Mercury Signatures	39
Chapter Four	HMLR Acceptance of Electronic Signatures on Deeds – Conveyancer-Certified Electronic Signatures	49
Chapter Five	Relevant Case Law	87
Chapter Six	Risk Management	107
Chapter Seven	The Future	129
Appendix	Resources	137

INTRODUCTION

'Can I sign a contract on behalf of my client? What are the risks?'

'What is an electronic signature and is it legally valid?'

'What are Mercury signatures and conveyancer-certified electronic signatures and what are HMLR's requirements?'

'How do I start to look at the risks of choosing a platform provider?'

These are some of the everyday questions that conveyancers ask themselves which this Practical Guide will answer. It is intended to be a handy reference guide to some of the most common issues arising in relation to signing deeds and contracts for the sale and purchase of land. HMLR requirements will be highlighted and sample signature clauses will be provided.

The conveyancing landscape is moving quickly and nowhere more so than in relation to document signing. For years, conveyancers simply asked their clients to sign the contract and to sign a transfer, mortgage deed or lease in the presence of an independent witness who would sign and add their name, address and occupation as evidence that they had witnessed the signature of the party to the deed. That world rapidly changed with HMLR's announcement on 27 July 2020 that it would accept witnessed electronic signatures on deeds. On 28 March 2022, HMLR consolidated its practice and advice again and introduced a new Practice Guide and changed the terminology from 'witnessed electronic signatures' to 'conveyancer-certified electronic signatures'. Some of the practical issues and risks will be considered, along with the HMLR guidance and what appears to be the current view of the lenders.

The law and practice relating to document signing is complex and differing procedures can be adopted across practice areas. For example, those concluding commercial transactions with an international element have used signatures generated electronically for some time. This Practical Guide will focus on the issues of particular relevance to conveyancing transactions in England and Wales.

There is a lot of detail and guidance available for practitioners who want to know more about the background or legal status of electronic signatures. Some of the key work and guidance from the Law Commission, the Law Society and the EU is referred to in the 'resources' section.

Throughout this Practical Guide, conveyancers will be prompted to consider practical issues and risks under the heading 'Practice Points'.

The term 'conveyancer' is used to describe fee earners, whether qualified or not who have conduct of conveyancing transactions.

The law is believed to be correct and up to date as at 25 June 2022.

CHAPTER ONE

WHAT IS A SIGNATURE?

This Practical Guide considers the implications for conveyancers of HMLR's acceptance of conveyancer-certified electronic signatures. Before we consider the details of how this will work in practice, this chapter will consider what amounts to a signature and the legal status of the electronic signature.

'What is a signature?' may seem like a very obvious question, but there are a wide range of actions capable of constituting a 'signature'. It is generally accepted to mean the physical act of someone writing their own name, in the same way, each time they sign a document. However, a signature does not have to involve writing a name; it could be making a mark or putting a cross on the page. The method used to sign a document is important – it usually requires the signatory to use a pen to make an indelible mark (as opposed to a pencil, for example) and this is what would be described as a 'wet ink' signature and is the form of signature with which conveyancers are most familiar. The FCA described it neatly as: 'signing a document by hand using a pen'.

The wet ink signature has been an integral part of the conveyancing process for a long time. In addition to being the means by which a buyer or seller will indicate their acceptance to the contents of a document, in more recent times it has also served as an additional tool in the conveyancer's risk management armoury. Typically, as part of the firm's due diligence processes, a conveyancer will take a copy from an original document provided by the client (usually a passport or driving licence) which in addition to giving a photographic representation as to the likeness of the client, contains a signature against which the conveyancers should then check subsequent signatures purporting to be those of the client.

The production of a passport as part of the identification procedures is not fool proof and there are weaknesses to the wet ink signature process which will be considered in Chapter 6.

Having established that a signature does not have to be made in wet ink and use the name of the signatory at all, it is then necessary to consider the purpose of signing a document at all. This is widely accepted and well known in that the purpose of asking someone to put their name to a document is:

- for the signatory to indicate their acceptance of the terms of that document; and
- to confirm that they have read and understood the document; and
- to confirm their intention to be bound by the terms of that document

Terminology

Before we move on to consider conveyancer-certified electronic signatures in detail, it is necessary to clarify various terms. The terms 'digital signature' and 'electronic signature' are often used to mean the same thing, but they are different. Broadly, 'electronic signatures' is an umbrella term which includes digital signatures. Electronic signatures use an electronic process to act as the acceptance by the signatory of an online document, record or agreement. This is not necessarily a completely secure process, particularly if unencrypted email is part of the process.

An electronic signature might involve the signatory:

- 'Signing' their name with their usual signature with a stylus or finger to signify acceptance
- Typing their name at the bottom of a document
- Using a scan of their signature that has previously been written in wet ink
- Clicking a button on a website to denote acceptance
- Using a web-based e-signature platform

If a more secure method of electronic signature is required, a digital signature will be used. This uses encryption to ensure authentication. Providers may use Public Key Infrastructure (PKI) technology in the creation of their digital signature platform. In its simplest terms, PKI requires an algorithm to produce two 'keys' – these are long numbers, one of which is public and one private. Digital signatures essentially link these keys to prove authenticity. For more explanation, go to Appendix 7 of the 'Electronic Execution of Documents: Industry Working Group Interim Report (01.02.2022)'.

As indicated in the introduction, this Practical Guide is not aiming to give a detailed explanation of the complex technological steps required to create safe signature processes by electronic means. Such explanations are beyond the scope of this book and the knowledge of the writer. However, when sourcing a platform provider, conveyancers should ensure that they understand the process used to create the signature platform and are satisfied, to the extent possible, as to security and authentication.

HMLR refers to various forms of electronic signature as follows:

Mercury signatures

This is a basic form of electronic signature in that it allows for a signature page to be signed in wet ink (in the physical presence of witness). The signature page will then be captured with a scanner or camera and is sent back to the conveyancer by a single email which includes the scanned signature page and a copy of the final agreed document, the terms of which that signature is accepting. See Chapter 3.

Conveyancer-certified electronic signatures

This is the replacement within a standard deed (typically a transfer) of a wet ink signature with an electronic signature. From July 2020 to March 2022 these were referred to as 'witnessed electronic signatures'. A witness must still be present at the time the signatory adds their electronic signature. The witness must also 'sign' electronically. For HMLR purposes this form of signature requires two factor authentication and is the form of electronic signature on deeds which HMLR confirmed that it would accept on 27 July 2020. This Practical Guide focuses on this aspect. See Chapter 4.

Qualified electronic signatures

This is a form of signature operating on the basis that a Qualified Trust Service Provider has standards in place to securely and accurately verify the identity of the signatory which protects the integrity of the document. This is a more secure form of signing as the identification checking and encryption are carried out to a specified standard which is controlled by a regulated body. This form of signature is not yet accepted by HMLR. See Chapter 7.

Platform/platform provider

The HMLR guidance on conveyancer-certified electronic signatures refers to a 'platform'. In this context it refers in generic terms to an electronic system for the delivery and management of information including, of course, conveyancing documents. As mentioned later in this Practical Guide, HMLR will not endorse any particular platform or provider; conveyancers must research the market and source a provider which meets their needs. In this Practical Guide, we will refer to 'platform provider' to mean the commercial organisation which a firm will choose to provide a system enabling conveyancer-certified electronic signatures of deeds that meets specific HMLR requirements.

Deed/transfer

This Practical Guide is considering a form of electronic signature which is specifically mandated by HMLR and is specific to the conveyancing process in England and Wales. This Practical Guide will outline which deeds HMLR will accept for registration purposes signed in this manner but for the most part it is likely to be the transfer which is signed using conveyancer-certified electronic signatures thus, for ease of reference, this is the document which we will refer to as typically being signed in this way.

Note that HMLR would accept a mortgage deed signed using a conveyancer-certified electronic signature, but it is not clear that the lenders will yet agree to this. For more information, see Chapter 4.

Note also that Lasting Powers of Attorney cannot be signed using a conveyancer-certified electronic signature.

Are electronic signatures legally valid?

Having established in broad terms the definition of an electronic signature, let's move on to consider whether electronic signatures are legally valid.

Law Society

In the Practice Notes referred to in the 'resources' section the Law Society concluded that:

> *'The Law Commission published the conclusions of its work in the autumn of 2019 and confirmed that an electronic signature is capable in law of being used to execute documents (including deeds). This was helpful as it corroborated the view we previously expressed in the e-signature practice note.*
>
> *The Law Commission emphasised the need for authentication and the need to follow formalities of execution, and highlighted that the courts have previously held that simple markings such as an 'X' made by the hand of the maker may constitute a valid and binding signature.*
>
> *In many cases, execution by means of an authenticated electronic signature will deliver much greater transactional certainty and security than means of execution previously upheld by the courts.*
>
> *However, at the time of writing there is no definitive statement from a higher court upholding electronic signatures and, in the absence of a court decision or primary legislation, there remains an inconsistent approach to the use of electronic signatures.*
>
> *The Law Commission has recommended a review of the law of deeds and suggested that government may wish to consider codifying the law on electronic signatures in order to improve the accessibility of the law.'*
>
>

Law Commission

The acceptance of witnessed electronic signatures in July 2020 in the midst of a global pandemic was driven to some extent by the latter and the need for conveyancers to have some flexibility as to how clients signed deeds submitted for registration, but much of the groundwork had been done by the Law Commission. Practitioners who are interested in this area more generally should read the influential report released on 4 September 2019. The following are what the Law Commission described as the 'high level conclusions' of their report, which focussed on two key aspects of the electronic execution of documents, namely:

1. *the use of electronic signatures to execute documents where there is a statutory requirement that a document must be "signed"; and*

2. *the electronic execution of deeds, including the requirements of witnessing and attestation and delivery.*

Notably the report did not include wills nor to registered dispositions under the LRA 2002. We will see that HMLR has moved on since the Law Commission published its report (and will signing is outside the scope of this book).

Statement of the law: execution with an electronic signature

'An electronic signature is capable in law of being used to execute a document (including a deed) provided that

(i) the person signing the document intends to authenticate the document and

(ii) any formalities relating to execution of that document are satisfied.

Such formalities may be required under a statute or statutory instrument, or may be laid down in a contract or other private law instrument under which a document is to be executed. The following are examples of formalities that might be required: (i) that the signature be witnessed; or (ii) that the signature be in a specified form (such as being handwritten).

An electronic signature is admissible in evidence in legal proceedings. It is admissible, for example, to prove or disprove the identity of a signatory and/or the signatory's intention to authenticate the document.

Save where the contrary is provided for in relevant legislation or contractual arrangements, or where case law specific to the document in question leads to a contrary conclusion, the common law adopts a pragmatic approach and does not prescribe any particular form or type of signature. In determining whether the method of signature adopted demonstrates an authenticating intention the courts adopt an objective approach considering all of the surrounding circumstances.

The Courts have, for example, held that the following non-electronic forms amount to valid signatures:

- *signing with an 'X';*
- *signing with initials only;*
- *using a stamp of a handwritten signature;*
- *printing of a name;*
- *signing with a mark, even where the party executing the mark can write; and*
- *a description of the signatory if sufficiently unambiguous, such as "Your loving mother" or "Servant to Mr Sperling".*

Electronic equivalents of these non-electronic forms of signature are likely to be recognised by a court as legally valid. There is no reason in principle to think otherwise.

The courts have, for example, held that the following electronic forms amount to valid signatures in the case of statutory obligations to provide a signature where the statute is silent as to whether an electronic signature is acceptable:

- *a name typed at the bottom of an email;*

- *clicking an "I accept" tick box on a website; and*
- *the header of a SWIFT message.*

With specific regard to deeds and the witnessing requirements thereof, a deed must be signed in the physical presence of a witness who attests the signature. This is the case even where both the person executing the deed and the witness are executing / attesting the document using an electronic signature.'

eIDAS Regulation

Another important factor governing the development of the use of electronic signatures in conveyancing is the Regulation (EU) 910/2014 on electronic identification and trust services for electronic transactions in the internal market. It came into force on 1 July 2016. At the moment at least, as a European regulation, it has direct effect in UK law and automatically applies in the UK. The ICO website contains useful information and detail about the Regulation. The basic premise behind the Regulation is to give a framework allowing European citizens to use electronic identification to access online public services in other EU member states.

The impact which leaving the EU might have is difficult to assess. However, HMLR is working on Qualified Electronic Signatures and the eIDAS Regulation is informing that work. Conveyancers who are interested should consider signing up to HMLR email updates and responding to future consultations.

Conclusion

The weight of commentary in favour of an electronic signature to a document being legally valid is strong. It would be difficult to argue against the Law Commission's proposition that *'an electronic signature is capable in law of being used to execute a document (including a deed)'*, in the absence of an allegation of fraud or error. However, it is worth noting that the higher courts have not considered the legal validity of electronic signatures, so there is always some room for doubt.

Signatory's intention

Central to the above conclusions as to validity of electronic signatures is that it must be possible to conclude from the conduct of the signatory that they *intended to authenticate* the document being signed electronically and thus be bound by its contents. A digital audit trail which can be created when using electronic signatures will generally be evidence of the intention of the signatory to authenticate and be bound by the document, although fraud, for example, would invalidate such intention.

HMLR

All of the above has led HMLR to conclude that conveyancer-certified electronic signatures are acceptable for deeds which are submitted for land registration purposes. This is the scope of this Practical Guide. When considering in a broader context whether a document signed by electronic means will be legally valid, practitioners will need to keep in mind the nature of the document, the signatory, any statutory requirements and jurisdictional issues. In this Practical Guide, we are considering the very specific issue of signing contracts and deeds for the sale of land In England and Wales. If there are any issues as to the location of signatories or whether the jurisdiction in which a document is electronically signed is valid, practitioners will have to carefully consider these points.

Additional content / commentary

This is an area about which a lot has been written and which is fast developing. The Law Society and other organisations have released useful guidance that is beyond the scope of this Practical Guide. A notable new addition to the reading list in this area is the 'Electronic Execution of Documents: Industry Working Group Interim Report (01.02.2022)'. The objectives of this Report are very relevant:

(a) to analyse the current situation in England and Wales

(b) to set out simple best practice guidance which can followed immediately, using existing technology, and

(c) to make recommendations for future analysis and reform

In the light of the comments in the next chapter about the increasing practice of not sending a hard copy of a contract post exchange, conveyancers will be particularly interested to note the first principle of best practice put forward in the Report: *'Agree as early as possible that a document is to be executed electronically and the procedure for doing so.* The Report contains a useful summary at Appendix 3 of the electronic execution requirements for common document types and Appendix 4 contains a table for formalities for common types of transaction.

CHAPTER TWO

THE CONTRACT AND DEEDS IN CONVEYANCING

This chapter will cover the requirements to create a valid contract and deed relating to the transfer of land in England and Wales. It will also cover some of the more common attestation clauses suggested by HMLR and a reminder on witnessing requirements.

Contracts in conveyancing

In its broadest sense, a contract is a document whereby the parties to that document agree to be bound by its terms. To be valid, a contract must include:

- offer
- acceptance
- consideration
- intention to create legal relations

The above are the standard requirements for any contract in England and Wales and any contract for the sale of land must involve those key elements. A contract for the sale of land has extra requirements due to the unique nature of land and the need for certainty when contracting. The vast majority of conveyancers will use the Law Society's contract incorporating the Standard Conditions of Sale (5th edition – 2018 revision).

The conveyancing transaction has become very process driven, meaning that the transaction is highly mechanised and commoditised with many firms using case management systems and apps which help streamline the process. This can often involve the use of standard forms including the contract, many of which are auto completed. There is no doubt that this assists firms in terms of efficiency and profitability but it does mean that conveyancers can lose sight of the importance of the creation of a contract for the sale and purchase of a piece of land. This is not a contract for the sale of a commodity which can be replaced or recreated if something goes wrong with the performance of the contract. By definition, land is a finite resource and every contract involving land, however small the parcel of land involved, is for land which does not exist anywhere else on earth.

Thus, certainty when dealing with contracts for the sale of land is essential. It is important to minimise the risk of a contract for the sale of land being created by exchange of letters or orally, for example. For this reason, in addition to the above elements required to create a valid contract, the Law of Property (Miscellaneous Provisions) Act 1989 provides as follows:

> ***2. Contracts for sale etc. of land to be made by signed writing.***
>
> *(1) A contract for the sale or other disposition of an interest in land can only be made in writing and only by incorporating all the terms which the parties have expressly agreed in one document or, where contracts are exchanged, in each.*
>
> *(2) The terms may be incorporated in a document either by being set out in it or by reference to some other document.*
>
> *(3) The document incorporating the terms or, where contracts are exchanged, one of the documents incorporating them (but not necessarily the same one) must be signed by or on behalf of each party to the contract.*

In a nutshell, this means that a contract for the sale and purchase of a piece of land in England and Wales must be in writing and must incorporate all the agreed terms.

s 2 allows for the contract to be in two parts which are in identical format. This is why it is important for conveyancers to follow the Law Society's formulae for exchange when exchanging by telephone. The conveyancers should go through the terms of the contract to ensure that each part is identical. This is particularly important where there are additional provisions, clauses and riders added to the contract in question. It is of equal importance to ensure that this conversation and the content of any riders are comprehensively and accurately recorded in the conveyancer's memorandum of exchange.

Deeds in conveyancing

Generally, a legal interest in land cannot be conveyed or created without a deed as set out in s 52(1) LPA 1925. An assent is one of the exceptions but all must be properly signed and witnessed.

To be a deed the document must:

- be in writing
- make it clear on the face of it that it is intended to be a deed by the person making it all the parties to it. This can be done by the document describing itself as a deed or expressing itself to be executed as a deed 'or otherwise'
- be validly executed as a deed by the person making it or by one or more of the parties to it (1989 Act)

Note that it is no longer a legal requirement that a deed is signed under a seal (s 1 (1)(b) 1989 Act).

s 1(2) 1989 Act states:

> *1 (2) An instrument shall not be a deed unless—*
>
> *(a) it makes it clear on its face that it is intended to be a deed by the person making it or, as the case may be, by the parties to it (whether by describing itself as a deed or expressing itself to be executed or signed as a deed or otherwise); and*
>
> *(b) it is validly executed as a deed by that person or, as the case may be, one or more of those parties.*

Common types of deed in conveyancing

- transfer (TR1)
- transfer of part (TP1)
- transfer of a charge or portfolio of charges (TR4)
- transfer of portfolio of titles (whole or part)
- cancellation of entries relating to a registered charge (DS1)
- release of part of the land from a registered charge (DS3)

All of the above are HMLR prescribed forms.

Other deeds include:

- some forms of lease
- deed of easement
- deed of variation
- mortgage deed
- conveyance

The execution (signature) requirements are as follows:

> *s (1) (3) An instrument is validly executed as a deed by an individual if, and only if—*
>
> *(a) it is signed—*
>
> *(i) by him in the presence of a witness who attests the signature; or*
>
> *(ii) at his direction and in his presence and the presence of two witnesses who each attest the signature; and*

(b) it is delivered as a deed

So, for execution of deeds by individuals, we must have three distinct elements:

1. signature
2. attestation
3. delivery

Let's look at each of these in turn.

1. Signature

s 1(4) makes it clear that signing includes 'making one's mark on the instrument and 'signature' is to be construed accordingly'. Thus, as with signing a contract, it is not necessary for a signature to be in the form of someone's name provided that they have made their mark on the deed and that their signature is appropriately witnessed. We have seen in Chapter 1 that an electronic signature is, in the opinion of the Law Society and the Law Commission, highly likely to constitute a valid signature to a deed. In Chapter 4, we will consider HMLR's specific requirements relating to deeds submitted for registration using conveyancer-certified electronic signatures.

2. Attestation

Each individual signing a deed must do so 'in the presence of a witness who attests the signature' (s 1(3) 1989 Act). Broadly, attestation is the act of the witnessing by an independent person of the signing of a deed by the signatory. This is followed by the witness signing the deed as well to verify that it was properly signed by those who are bound by the content of the deed. Each signature must be witnessed. We will see that this is an essential feature of signing a deed and is also a central requirement of signing using the Mercury signature process and conveyancer-certified electronic signatures.

In its simplest form, the signatory and the witness must be together at the time the deed is signed and the witness must see the signature taking place (whether this is a wet ink signature or an electronic signature).

3. Delivery

The third element required when an individual is executing a document is delivery. It must be 'delivered as a deed'. This means that the signatory expressly or impliedly, by words or conduct, and intention to be bound by the provisions in the deed.

If a conveyancer is acting in relation to the creation or disposal of an interest in land, and they purport to deliver a document as a deed on behalf of a party to it, there is a conclusive presumption in favour of a buyer that the conveyancer is authorised to deliver it (s 1(5) 1989 Act).

Examples of attestation clauses

There is no legally prescribed format of an attestation clause (that is, the signature clause). The important thing is to ensure that the clause makes it clear that the signatures of the parties to the deed are intended to execute the document and that they were made in the presence of the witnesses. It should also be clear that the document has been executed 'as a deed'. If there are any variations to the signing process, it would be prudent to alter the attestation clause to reflect the circumstances of signature. Practitioners may also wish to add the occupation of the witness. HMLR PG8 gives a number of examples, the most common of which are:

Deed signed by an individual

Signed as a deed by (insert full name of individual)
in the presence of:
Signature...
signature of witness..
witness name (in block capitals)..................................
witness address...

Assent signed by an individual

Signed by (insert full name of individual)
in the presence of:
Signature...
signature of witness..
witness name (in block capitals)..................................
witness address...

Deed signed by person unable to read or understand the deed

If a signatory does not understand the nature of the document or the purpose of signing, it may be that they do not have any capacity to sign the document at all. However, if the signatory is not literate, the contents could be read to them or the effect of it explained. If they cannot read the document, it might be read out to them or a braille copy be made available. If English is not the signatory's first language, it could be translated.

In any of these circumstances, best practice demands that the conveyancer witnesses the signature and amends the attestation clause accordingly. The conveyancer should also keep a contemporaneous note of the circumstances of the signing and perhaps consider, in addition, keeping a video recording (albeit the firm would need to properly consider process and risk in this instance). HMLR will accept the following wording without the need for the conveyancer to obtain prior approval:

> Signed as a deed by (full name of individual) in the presence of the undersigned, [he][she] having first confirmed that [he][she] had familiarised [himself][herself] with its contents by (state method used):
>
> Signature..
>
> *signature of witness*..
>
> *witness name (in block capitals)*.................................
>
> *witness address*..

Rule 206(3) LRR 2003 allows a different attestation clause to be used but if the prescribed wording is not going to be followed, best practice demands that the buyer's conveyancer seeks agreement from HMLR as to the form of wording prior to exchange of contracts. This highlights the importance to the buyer's conveyancer of ensuring that the form of transfer is agreed at an early stage.

Signatory physically unable to sign

If a person cannot physically sign a deed, it will be validly executed if it is signed at their direction and in the presence of two witnesses who each attest the signature (s 1(3)(a)(ii) 1989 Act). HMLR accepts the following:

Signed as a deed by (full name of person signing) at the direction and on behalf of (full name of individual) in [his][her] presence and in the presence of:

Sign here the name of the individual and your own name, e.g., John Smith by Jane Brown.........................

Signature of first witness..................................

name (in block capitals)..................................

Address...

Signature of second witness............................

name (in block capitals)..................................

address...

Execution of deeds by companies registered under the Companies Acts

s 44 2006 Act came into force on 6 April 2008 and applies to deeds executed on or after that date by companies registered under previous Companies Acts and those registered in Northern Ireland. A deed must be validly executed by a company.

The two main methods by which a document can be executed by a company are either:

1. by affixing the company's common seal, or

2. by the signature on behalf of the company of either (i) two of the company's directors or one director and the company secretary or (ii) a director of the company in the presence of a witness who attests the director's signature

A company can appoint an attorney under a power of attorney to execute a deed on its behalf.

S 44 states that:

> *(1) Under the law of England and Wales or Northern Ireland a document is executed by a company–*
>
> *(a) by the affixing of its common seal, or*
>
> *(b) by signature in accordance with the following provisions.*
>
> *(2) A document is validly executed by a company if it is signed on behalf of the company–*
>
> *(a) by two authorised signatories, or*
>
> *(b) by a director of the company in the presence of a witness who attests the signature.*
>
> *(3) The following are 'authorised signatories' for the purposes of subsection (2)–*
>
> *(a) every director of the company, and*
>
> *(b) in the case of a private company with a secretary or a public company, the secretary (or any joint secretary) of the company…*

Execution under seal

Normally the seal will be affixed to the deed in the presence of the company secretary and one director or, two directors who attest the sealing by signing the deed and describing themselves by their office (i.e., that of secretary or director). Remember that mere sealing of a document will not convert it into a deed. It must be clear on the face of the document that it is intended to be so. HMLR therefore requires the following:

Executed as a deed by affixing the common seal of (name of company) in the presence of: Signature of director.. Signature of [director] [secretary]...

Conveyancers acting for a buyer from a company should agree the form of transfer well in advance of exchange of contracts and should look carefully at the proposed attestation clause. The Articles of Association of most companies authorise affixing the company seal to a deed in the presence of people other than a director and the secretary. The buyer's conveyancer will want to ensure that the buyer takes the protection of s 74 (1) LPA 1925 (as amended) which states that:

> ***74. Execution of instruments by or on behalf of corporations.***
>
> *(1) In favour of a purchaser an instrument shall be deemed to have been duly executed by a corporation aggregate if a seal purporting to be the corporation's seal purports to be affixed to the instrument in the presence of and attested by—*
>
> > *(a) two members of the board of directors, council or other governing body of the corporation, or*
> >
> > *(b) one such member and the clerk, secretary or other permanent officer of the corporation or his deputy*

Thus, if the deed is executed by a company affixing the seal in the presence of persons other than a director and the secretary or two directors, HMLR may ask for evidence that the people attesting are authorised by the company's Articles to do so. HMLR may also request a certified copy of the appropriate board resolution. In this instance therefore the buyer's conveyancer should request this information prior to exchange of contracts or at the very least, prior to completion to ensure that HMLR does not raise a requisition on receipt of the application for registration.

Execution by company other than under a common seal

S 44(2)(a) and (3) 2006 Act protects a buyer (including a lessee, mortgagee or other person who for valuable consideration acquires an interest in property) if the following attestation clause is used in a deed which is executed on or after 6 April 2008:

Executed as a deed by (name of company) acting by [a director and its secretary] [two directors] Signature of director.. Signature of [secretary] [director]....................................

Since 20 September 2019, HMLR has not accepted 'signed as a deed' as an acceptable form of wording in prescribed form deeds executed by companies and limited liability partnerships. Where a disposal is in a prescribed form that must be executed as a deed (for example, a TR1) HMLR requires that the form of execution set out in schedule 9 to the LRR 2003 is used as above.

Under s 44 (2)(b) 2006 Act, a company may execute a document under the law of England and Wales or Northern Ireland by a single director if that signature is witnessed and attested and the following attestation clause must be used:

Executed as a deed by (name of company) acting by a director in the presence of: Signature of director... *signature of witness*.. *name (in block capitals)*.. *address*..

PG8 gives a number of other examples of attestation clauses for particular situations including non-registered companies, overseas companies, LLPs, charities, administrative receivers, liquidators and execution under a power of attorney.

Witnessing Practice Points

As mentioned above, the requirements under s 1(3)(b) 1989 Act and s 44(2)(b) 2006 Act are that the witness must be in the physical presence of the signatory of the deed, even if an electronic signature is being used. Very importantly, therefore, witnessing cannot take place by virtual or remote means. Thus, witnessing by a remote video link (e.g., Skype or zoom) is not sufficient because the signatory and the witness are not in each other's physical presence at the time of signing. The witness and the signatory could be separated by glass to maintain social distancing, for example, looking through a car or house window – the fundamental point is that the witness must be able to see the signatory signing the document in their physical presence.

There are some basic points which are relevant to witnessing. Most conveyancers will attempt to explain the process of signature and witnessing to their clients and signatories in the simplest possible terms. For example:

'Please arrange to sign the enclosed document where your initials appear in between the pencil crosses. Please ensure that you sign in the presence of an adult, independent witness. This means that the witness must not be:

- a party to the deed
- your partner, spouse or civil partner
- a relation of yours
- the partner, spouse or civil partner of any other party to the deed
- a relation of any other party to the deed

Once your witness has watched you sign, they must immediately sign their name and print their name address and occupation where indicated on the document.

If there is more than one party who needs to sign the deed, their signatures also need to be witnessed as indicated above. Each signature must be separately witnessed. The same person can witness all signatures provided they sign their name and include the details as above for every signature.

The witness must be present when each person signs.

Plans

If there is a plan attached to the document, every party to the document should check the plan carefully to ensure that it is correct. If it is correct, each party to the deed must sign the plan. The witness must not sign the plan.

Please do not date the document and return it as soon as possible.

If you have any questions about how to sign and witness the document, please contact me to discuss prior to signing it.'

HMLR checks on witnessing

When a document is received for registration, HMLR will check:

- that the signature is in ink or indelible medium
- that a witness has signed the deed
- that their signature clearly records the witnessing of the signing of the deed by each individual concerned
- that the name and address of the witness appear in legible form on the deed (to allow the witness to be traced should any questions later arise concerning execution)
- that each signature has been separately attested

- if the same witness has witnessed each individual signature, HMLR will check that each signature has been separately attested unless it is absolutely clear by express wording on the face of the attestation that the witness is witnessing both or all signatures in the presence of the named signatories

If a document is not correctly signed and witnessed, it will be rejected by HMLR which will inevitably prompt a requisition and delay.

However, all conveyancers will be only too aware of the mistakes which parties are capable of making when arranging to sign and witness documents. It is for this reason that many buyers' conveyancers will now request a copy of the undated but signed transfer preferably prior to exchange of contracts but at the very least prior to completion to enable them to be satisfied that the transfer has been properly signed and witnessed. If the buyer's conveyancer only discovers after completion that the signing and witnessing procedures have not been properly followed, this can seriously compromise a registration. Thus, requesting a copy of the signed transfer prior to completion is a straightforward risk management tool. Some seller's conveyancers reject this request citing the possibility of fraud as a risk. They are presumably suggesting that the buyer's conveyancer might seek to fraudulently register a transfer of the title before actual completion. This argument is not convincing. If the seller's conveyancer provides an uncertified, undated photocopy of the signed (and witnessed) transfer with the word 'copy' written across each page, it is hard to see how this could be presented for registration.

Note that the Protocol states that the seller's conveyancer will provide the buyer's conveyancer with a copy of the transfer executed by the seller after exchange of contracts and before completion. The buyer's conveyancer then has the chance to check the execution of the copy transfer that has been supplied (Protocol, para 24).

Other witnessing basics

- A party to the deed cannot witness the signature of another party to the deed.

- HMLR will expect to see on the face of the deed that the witness has signed it, and has added their name and address (plus postcode) in legible form.

- Some conveyancers may also require the witness to add their occupation but HMLR does not require this. However, this is a prudent step to assist with locating the witness should questions arise after completion regarding execution of the deed.

- The same witness may witness each individual signature but each signature must be separately attested (unless it is clear by express wording on the face of the attestation that the witness is witnessing both or all signatures in the presence of the named signatories). Best advice for conveyancers is to ensure that the witness has signed and printed their details in full beneath *every* signature which they have attested.

- Most conveyancers will specify that an 'independent person' should witness the signature and that the spouse, civil partner, cohabitee or a member of the signatory's family should not witness the signature. However, there is no legislation preventing such a person witnessing a signature but it is best avoided.

- Similarly, it is advisable that the witness be aged 18 or over or is sufficiently mature for their evidence to be relied on if the circumstances of signature are ever questioned in the future.

- However, it is worth noting that with the practical difficulties of social distancing which have become necessary during 2020 due to the Covid-19 pandemic, some signatories may have had little choice but to involve members of their family in witnessing documents.

This is another reason why it is advisable for the buyer's conveyancer to see a copy of the signed attestation clauses prior to completion. If it is clear that a member of the signatory's family for example, has witnessed the signature, the buyer's conveyancer may wish to obtain details from the seller's conveyancer as to the circumstances of signing in case HMLR should raise a requisition. A very risk averse conveyancer may also seek an undertaking from the seller's conveyancer to assist promptly and at the seller's expense with any such requisition.

Methods for signing contracts and deeds

Face-to-face meeting

The conveyancer could meet their client face-to-face to explain the significance of the contract, mortgage deed and transfer and arrange for the client to sign in wet ink at that meeting. This approach has generally been accepted as the 'gold standard' for signing documents because, in theory, it enables the conveyancer to:

- meet the client and, if necessary, check that the client resembles their identification documents
- check that the client's signature matches that on the identification documents
- talk to the client about the transaction/their intentions etc, as part of the 'know your client' process
- explain the nature and effect of the documents being signed to the client
- witness the client's signature

Posting the documents

However, more streamlined work processes and the effect of Covid-19 means that in most conveyancing transactions, the conveyancer will send the documents to their client and will invite the client to add a wet ink signature and have their signature witnessed as appropriate and will ask the client to return the document/s undated.

The conveyancer will usually include a letter or report when sending the document to a seller or buyer client which explains the significance of the document being signed. It is reasonably likely, therefore, that the client will understand the nature of the document that they are signing because they have received a hardcopy of the relevant document with an explanatory letter and have taken time to sign the document with a wet ink signature.

Conveyancers should check the client's signature on the document against the identification documents held but generally, this has been seen by conveyancers as a reasonably safe method of securing their clients signature to the contract. Frankly, conveyancers may have become too complacent about posting documents to clients for signature. It would not be difficult for a determined fraudster to intercept a document in the post or simply to forge a signature. This conveyancing risk seems quite high, particularly if the conveyancer does not meet the client in question.

Someone else could sign the document on their client's behalf

Power of attorney

The contract, mortgage deed or transfer could be signed on behalf of the signatory by an attorney appointed by the donor under the terms of a power of attorney. It would be necessary to establish that the power had been validly granted. The Lender's Handbook has particular requirements in clause 5.17 about signing under a power of attorney and these plus any lender-specific Part 2 amendments must be complied with. However, the likelihood is that the document in question will be signed by the attorney in wet ink and witnessed if a deed. See also PG9 for detail on HMLR's requirements regarding powers of attorney.

Should the conveyancer sign the contract on the seller's behalf?

The conveyancer could sign the contract on the client's behalf. It has long been accepted that a conveyancer can sign a contract on their client's behalf as agent for the client without the need for a power of attorney, for example, to authorise this act. The conveyancer should, as a matter of best practice, seek their client's written authority to sign the contract. The risk is less about whether the signature by the conveyancer constitutes an acceptable signature, because invariably it does, but rather whether the conveyancer doing the signing should take the risk.

Warranty of authority, contract signing and *Dreamvar*

Conveyancers might be interested to note that one of the issues considered by the Court of Appeal in *Dreamvar (UK) Ltd v Mishcon de Reya and P & P Property Ltd v Owen White and Catlin LLP [2018] EWCA Civ 1082* ('*Dreamvar*') is the fact that one of the contracts in question was signed by a conveyancer of the firm on 'behalf' of the seller 'client' who, of course, turned out to be a fraudster. Conveyancers interested in the reasoning are invited to consider the judgement but the Court of Appeal held that the conveyancer *'did indeed give a warranty that she was authorised to act on behalf of the actual [seller] who owned [the property]'* [para 56].

As it happens, in the *Dreamvar* case, the claim for breach of warranty of authority failed because the buyer's conveyancer had not placed any *reliance* on the fact that the conveyancer acting for the fraudulent seller had signed the contract on their behalf. For there to be inducement by the warranty, it must be relied upon. Fundamentally, the conveyancer's signature of the contract on behalf of the fraudulent seller had no material impact in terms of inducing the buyer to enter into the contract. But it clearly demonstrates that in so doing, the seller's conveyancer could face a claim of breach of warranty of authority in the event that something goes wrong or there is fraud.

Do not forget the wider issue for conveyancers that arose from *Dreamvar*, namely that, by confirming they act for the seller, a seller's conveyancer is warranting to the buyer's conveyancer that they act for the *'person/s who will be at the point of completion entitled to convey the legal and/or equitable title to the property'*. (that is, the true owner of the property). This position was reinforced by the Law Society's changes to the Code for Completion by Post in 2019.

Practice Points

A buyer's conveyancer should establish prior to exchange of contracts who will be signing the contract: is it the seller or the conveyancer signing on behalf of the seller? If the latter, the buyer's conveyancer may wish to follow up this discovery with written confirmation that they are relying on the signature of the contract by the seller's conveyancer as giving a warranty which will be relied upon. Clearly if a seller's conveyancer receives such communication, they should resist this assertion. Many conveyancers would therefore consider that it is too great a risk to sign the contract on their client's behalf and should make arrangements for the seller to sign either with a wet ink signature or an electronic one.

If the seller's conveyancer signs the contract on behalf of their client, they must have their client's express authority to do so. Once that authority is given, it does allow the solicitor to proceed to exchange. The authority can be given orally.

What safeguards should conveyancers put in place in the event that they decide to sign the contract on their client's behalf?

- They should obtain the express written authority of *all* sellers

- The consequences of allowing the conveyancer to sign the contract and proceed to exchange should be explained to all sellers in writing and in language that they can understand

- If the sellers have signed and returned the contract in readiness for exchange, it is still essential to obtain the irrevocable authority of all sellers to proceed to exchange on the day of exchange itself

- If a conveyancer signs the contract on behalf of a client company, the conveyancer should be satisfied that the company has been properly incorporated

If the seller's conveyancer does not obtain authority from their seller client to sign the contract on their behalf, this could lead to a claim for breach of warranty of authority resulting in a damages award against the conveyancer. Best practice demands that conveyancers do not sign the contract on behalf of their seller client. Managing this risk is especially important where a firm employs a large team of conveyancers.

What are the risks for the buyer's conveyancer?

On or before the day of exchange, the buyer's conveyancer may wish to contact the seller's conveyancer to establish whether the seller's conveyancer holds an original contract with a wet ink signature by the seller (and any occupiers). If the seller's conveyancer only holds a scanned copy of the contract showing the sellers wet ink signature, the buyer's conveyancer should establish what were the circumstances of the signing and scanning process. They may also wish to ask as to the whereabouts of the original contract with the wet ink signature. The buyer's conveyancer is entitled to be reasonably satisfied that the true seller has signed the contract. It is accepted that the buyer's conveyancer is entitled to rely on the warranty given by the seller's conveyancer confirming that they act for the true seller, but prevention must be better than cure in these circumstances. No conveyancer will want to find themselves relying on this warranty in the event of purchase money having been paid away to a fraudulent seller.

If the seller's conveyancer has signed the contract on behalf of their client, the buyer's conveyancer may wish to seek specific confirmation that the seller's authority has been properly obtained.

The above sets out some thoughts regarding the sale contract being signed on behalf of the seller as this is what arose in *Dreamvar*. But of course, the same considerations apply in relation to the purchase contract being signed by the conveyancer on behalf of their buyer client. However, given the significant consequences and potential losses that a buyer might incur if they default on the contract, it is hard to see why a buyer's conveyancer would want to take the risk and sign the contract on behalf of their client.

Electronic signature platform

When considering electronic signatures, it is important for the conveyancer to remember the nature of the document being signed. As an alternative to trying to secure wet ink signatures to documents, the conveyancers may consider using an electronic signature platform whereby their client is asked to 'sign' a document electronically. Many firms will do this regularly in relation to the Protocol forms (e.g., the Property Information Form or Fittings and Contents Form) and the contract itself. Note that such a platform may not meet HMLR's requirements set out in PG82 for conveyancer-certified electronic signatures.

We will consider in Chapter 3 signing deeds using Mercury signatures and in Chapter 4, signing deeds using conveyancer-certified electronic signatures.

Acceptance by conveyancers of contracts signed electronically

An increasing number of conveyancing firms are using document signing platforms and apps to streamline the process for completing and signing the Protocol forms and contracts. A question which is vexing some conveyancers is whether a conveyancer is *obliged* to accept a contract which has been signed electronically if they only find out from the other side that this is the method of signature *after* exchange of contracts. Many conveyancers still consider a contract signed by a seller or buyer in wet ink to be the 'gold standard' and are inclined to reject contracts presented to them which have been signed electronically. Additionally, some conveyancers are only sending scanned contracts by email following exchange of contracts, rather than a hard copy.

As we have seen in chapter 1, there seems little doubt that the addition of an electronic signature to a contract would be legally valid (subject to an allegation of fraud or other wrongdoing). Thus, if a hard copy of a contract which has been signed electronically is sent following exchange, there seems to be little doubt that the contract would be validly signed. If a conveyancer has concerns, they should find out prior to exchange how the contract is being signed and seek what they consider to be appropriate assurances in light of the answer given.

The second issue concerning conveyancers is what the position is where a conveyancer sends a scanned copy of the contract to the other side after exchange as an email attachment, rather than a hard copy. This could be a document on their system which has been signed using an electronic signature or a scanned copy the original of which has been signed by their client in wet ink. Many firms now scan hard copy documents and correspondence onto their case management system as a matter of course and destroy the originals.

The answer to this question is in the detail of the Formulae for Exchanging Contracts by Telephone – all three of the options contain implied undertakings:

> **Formula A** – *'Solicitors mutually agree that exchange shall take place from that moment and the solicitor holding both parts confirm that, as of that moment, he or she holds the part signed by his or her client(s) to the order of the other. He or she undertakes that day by first class post, or where the other solicitor is a member of a document exchange (as to which the inclusion of a reference thereto in the solicitor's letterhead shall be conclusive evidence) by delivery to that or any other affiliated exchange, or by hand delivery direct to that solicitor's office, to send his or her signed part of the contract to the other solicitor...'*

> **Formula B** – *'Each solicitor further undertakes that day by first class post, or, where the other solicitor is a member of a document exchange (as to the inclusion of a reference thereto in the solicitor's letterhead shall be conclusive evidence) by delivery to that or any other affiliated exchange, or by hand delivery direct to that solicitor's office, to send his or her signed part of the contract to the other...'*

> **Formula C** – *'Each solicitor undertakes to the other henceforth to hold the part of the contract in his or her possession to the other's order, so that contracts are exchanged at that moment, and to despatch it to the other on that day. ... 'To despatch' means to send by first class post, or, where the other solicitor is a member of a document exchange (as to which the inclusion of a reference thereto in the solicitor's letterhead is to be conclusive evidence) by delivery to that or any other affiliated exchange, or by hand delivery direct to the recipient solicitor's office.'*

So, a failure to send a hard copy of the contract (whether signed in wet ink or electronically) by post, DX or by hand to the other side following exchange of contracts amounts to a breach of undertaking. The simple fact is that the Formulae for Exchange have not yet been amended to allow for emailing electronic documents and, unless varied, they must be followed. Clearly if a firm is prepared to routinely breach these undertakings in the interests of electronic expediency, they must accept that they could leave themselves open to a claim for professional misconduct and/or a report to the Law Society, remembering that CQS accredited firms are obliged to follow the Protocol which incorporates the use of the Formulae for Exchange.

Conversely, those firms on the receiving end of a breach of undertaking must consider whether they are prepared to take any steps to try to enforce it and/or report non-compliance with the CQS to the Law Society.

Practice Points

If a firm is concerned to ensure that the conveyancer on the other side of the transaction is going to produce a contract signed by their client in wet ink, then they should raise an enquiry in this regard before exchange of contracts.

Similarly, if concerned, a firm should seek confirmation prior to exchange of contracts (if necessary, by way of undertaking) that the firm on the other side will dispatch a hard copy of the signed contract on the day of exchange in accordance with the undertaking contained in the Formulae for Exchange.

A further safeguard is to raise these questions on the telephone immediately before exchange of contracts. If a firm is concerned as to the method of signature of the contract or proposed dispatch, they could refuse to exchange contracts until agreement as to how to vary the Formulae for Exchange is reached. Clients should, of course, be kept up-to-date and any authority to exchange refreshed as appropriate.

If a conveyancing firm routinely obtains contracts signed electronically and only proposes to dispatch the contract via email post exchange, they should seek to vary the Formulae for Exchange or face the risk of an allegation of breach of undertaking. Professional courtesy surely demands this much.

There is little point in a firm of conveyancers seeking to circumvent these procedures by including a provision in the contract because the contract regulates the position as between seller and buyer and has no impact on the undertaking between conveyancers on exchange.

In the final analysis, if a disgruntled law firm is left holding a scanned copy of a contract which has been signed electronically following exchange of contracts, they should acknowledge receipt in writing and reaffirm their firm and their client's reliance on the statement contained within the Formulae for Exchange that each solicitor confirms that they hold a part of the contract in the agreed form signed by his or her client(s).

CHAPTER THREE

HMLR ACCEPTANCE OF ELECTRONIC SIGNATURES ON DEEDS – MERCURY SIGNATURES

HMLR's practice on the acceptance of electronic signatures on deeds moved very quickly during 2020. Early in the year, HMLR still took the view that any document which effects a registrable disposition and therefore requires to be completed by registration at HMLR pursuant to s27 LRA 2002 *cannot be signed electronically.* This included transfers, charges, registrable leases, the grant or reservation of easements and releases (s205(ii) LPA 1925).

However, in response to the impact of Covid-19, HMLR announced that from 4 May 2020 it would accept documents that had been signed using the Mercury signing approach. Less than three months later, it was announced that in addition, HMLR would accept deeds signed using a 'witnessed electronic signature'. In this chapter, we will consider the Mercury signing approach. This content was originally contained In PG8, but was moved to a newly created PG82 in March 2022.

HMLR and electronic signatures before 4 May 2020

HMLR accepted electronic signatures in limited circumstances prior to the acceptance of Mercury signatures and witnessed electronic signatures in 2020.

Digital mortgages

HMLR's position regarding the creation of digital mortgages remains unchanged. This is available on a limited basis. HMLR offers a digital mortgage service allowing property owners who are remortgaging only to sign the mortgage deed electronically. There are around 12 lenders using the service and five large volume conveyancing services that deal with bulk remortgage work. There are specific requirements for firms wishing to use the service. For further information, go to *HMLR: Sign your mortgage deed.*

HMLR has a 'lender services' policy which is governed by a Memorandum of Understanding to allow lenders to have direct access to the register to enable them to deal with electronic discharge of mortgages under the e-DS1 system. This is designed to meet the needs of lenders with portfolios of registered legal charges who wish to cancel charges from the register by means of an electronic form. This is not available in relation to 'day-to-day conveyancing' for firms.

Notices

There are various non-dispositionary deeds and documents that can be signed electronically, for example option agreements, pre-emption agreements, highways agreements, agreements the lease and contracts for sale. For example, if a contract signed electronically is sent to HMLR for noting on a title register by way of UN1 or AN1, HMLR will enter such a notice provided that any other requirements for the entry of a notice are satisfied. This is because the entry of a notice simply protects the priority of the relevant interest, and does not guarantee that the interest itself is valid (for more information see PG19). In this circumstance, it is not necessary for the electronically signed document to comply with the PG82 requirements (see Chapter 4).

Note as a matter of interest that Companies House will accept certified copies of charges executed using electronic means where they are submitted for registration via the Companies House web filing service.

Mercury signatures

What is a Mercury signature?

This is a form of signature of documents that was judicially recognised in a tax case: *R (on the application of Mercury Tax Group Ltd and another) v HMRC & Others [2008] EWHC 2721* ('the Mercury case'). In essence it is a method of signing which enables a document to be signed when all of the signatories are not physically present. A typical example would be where an international transaction needs to be concluded and it is not possible for them all to meet.

The Mercury signature procedure enables the conveyancer to complete a transaction on the basis that the transfer has been signed and witnessed in 'wet ink' in person; but instead of sending the original signed document, the signatory captures the signature page with a scanner or camera and emails the image (with the final version of the document) to the conveyancer who then combines the scanned signature page with the final version of the document. It is this capture of the original wet ink signature into a scanner or camera which 'converts' it into a form of electronic signature. This is the process referred to as 'option 1' in the Law Society's Practice Note: 'Execution of documents by virtual means'.

The use of Mercury signatures came back into the spotlight during the Covid-19 situation due to the challenges faced by conveyancers in relation to obtaining signed and witnessed documents for completion. The difficulty of staff working at home, offices being closed, no face-to-face appointments and clients self-isolating meant that more creative solutions to the signing of key conveyancing documents had to be found.

Can they be used for transfers?

The documents that can be Mercury signed in accordance with the process they refer to as 'option 1' (which is one of the processes laid out in the Mercury case and involves the return by email of the entire document and signed signature page) is helpfully laid out by HMLR in a table in Appendix 1 of PG82, but some of the most common are:

- A deed that effects one of the dispositions which are required to be completed by registration referred to in section 27(2) and (3) of the Land Registration Act 2002. The most commonly occurring deeds referred to in these sections are:

    - A transfer

    - A lease of more than 7 years (that is, a lease registrable at HMLR in its own right)

- A deed of easement
- A legal charge (mortgage)

- A discharge or release in form DS1 or form DS3
- Equivalent deeds in respect of unregistered land
- A power of attorney – other than a lasting power of attorney
- An assent of registered or unregistered land signed in accordance with option 1 – without Step 4 if the assent is not made by deed
- a deed of substituted security in respect of registered land, incorporating a discharge or release and a grant of a new charge, that has been electronically signed in this way, even though the discharge or release will not be in form DS1 or form DS3, provided there is nothing to prevent the deed from being regarded as sufficient proof of satisfaction of the charge (rule 114 (4) of the Land Registration Rules 2003)

What is the HMLR procedure?

The detail is contained in section 2 of PG82.

HMLR will accept the documents listed above for registration signed in accordance with option 1, as follows (section 2.2):

- *STEP 1 – Final agreed copies of the deed (including any plans) are emailed to each signing party by their conveyancer. To make clear what is expected (although this is not a requirement), conveyancers drafting the deed may wish to add a statement to the following effect, next to or beneath where the witness is to sign: "I confirm that I was physically present when [name of the party signing] signed this deed."*
- *STEP 2 – Each party prints the signature page only*

- *STEP 3 – Each party signs the signature page in the physical presence of a witness*
- *STEP 4 – The witness signs the signature page*
- *STEP 5 – Each party sends a single email to their conveyancer to which are attached the final agreed copy of the transfer (see STEP 1) and a PDF/JPEG or other suitable copy of the signed signature page*
- *STEP 6 – The conveyancing transaction is completed*
- *STEP 7 – The conveyancer applying for registration includes with the application the final agreed copy of the deed and the signed signature page or pages in the form of a single document.*

In STEP 1 and STEP 5, the conveyancer concerned can be a conveyancer other than the party's conveyancer provided that the arrangement has been agreed by all the parties' conveyancers.

In STEP 7, the combining of the deed and signature pages to include with the application to HM Land Registry may be done either by their being (i) electronically combined or (ii) printed out and then physically combined. The conveyancer must certify the resulting deed as a true copy of the original in the usual way. For this purpose, the 'original' is the final version of the deed and the signed signature page attached to the email to the conveyancer.

Note that the above process requires the signatory and the witness to print off the signature page and sign their names in pen (a 'wet ink' signature). The Mercury signature is technically an 'electronic' signature because the wet ink signature is scanned and sent to the conveyancer by email. The document is effective due to the association of the scanned copy of the wet ink signature with the document itself. It is not necessary therefore to request or obtain the original signed page from the signatory containing the wet ink signature.

The seller's conveyancer can combine the final version of the transfer document and signature page/s electronically or by printing off the final copy of the document and the scanned signature page – in both cases they will be combined as one document. They will then be able to date it in manuscript on the day of completion. The transfer will be sent to the buyer's conveyancer pursuant to the usual undertaking on completion who will then proceed with their registration, most often through the electronic Document Registration Service. Note however that the buyer's conveyancer can make the application in paper form.

If the transfer of part or other deed includes a plan, it must be signed by the transfer or other disponor (rule 213(2) LRR 2003). The conveyancer could sign the plan on their client's behalf (typed if necessary) or the signatory might type their name on the plan before returning this, plus the scanned signature page plus the original document back to their conveyancer. Whether acting for seller or buyer, both conveyancers should be satisfied that the appropriate authority was given if the conveyancer signs a plan on their client's behalf.

Section 2.3 of PG82 sets out the procedure for signing other documents using the Mercury signature process for example, application forms, statements of truth (but not statutory declarations) and various certificates. The main difference is that the signatory does not need to sign in the presence of a witness.

Practice points

Note that the process of using Mercury signatures must be agreed by both conveyancers at the outset. Thus, it would be prudent for a buyer's conveyancer to check with the seller's conveyancer as to the method of signature that will be adopted, especially if the buyer's conveyancer is not willing to accept a transfer signed in this manner.

Consider the risks – a key one to avoid is that the process is only used when the 'final agreed copy' of the transfer is emailed. The Mercury signature process cannot be used to add signature pages to a draft document.

A further weakness of this process is the fact that it relies on the use of email. Unless the firm is using encrypted email to send emails to clients and receive them, the cybercrime risk of email interception remains.

Evidence of process used

Conveyancers should consider what evidence they are going to retain on file to prove that the process above was used. For example:

- Written confirmation from both conveyancers that they agreed to adopt the process

- Retention of the email chain to demonstrate that the transfer is in its final, agreed form (step 1) and that the client returns the signature page back and the complete transfer in a single email (step 5)

- Consider having a video call so that the seller's conveyancer can confirm that the process was adopted, that the signatory is their client and that the witness was present (Step 3 and Step 4). If the video call is going to be recorded and retained or captured by screen shots, the parties involved must give data protection rights consent. Some may argue that conveyancers cannot be sure that their client has properly signed a transfer when it is sent to them in the traditional manner, but at least in that case the conveyancer has a hard copy of the deed in question with an original wet ink signature. In essence, the introduction of a remote electronic process increases the risk of fraud or simple human error

- The conveyancers confirming that completion has taken place (step 6). In practice, there is often very little communication between the conveyancers on the day of completion, other than a phone call to confirm receipt of the completion money and release of the keys. The Code for Completion by Post (2019) imposes an undertaking on the seller's conveyancer to confirm the date and time 'as soon as possible after completion' (para 13(ii)). Conveyancers should ensure that written evidence of this is properly embedded as part of their completion processes

Other steps to mitigate risk

The seller's conveyancer should check before completion is confirmed that the seller's scanned or photographed signature on the transfer is the same as that on the identification documents held on file for their seller client. Indeed, the buyer's conveyancer may insist that this is done.

Remember that the witness still needs to be physically present at the time the document is signed.

The conveyancers may wish to record in the 'additional provisions' section of the transfer that the document has been signed using the Mercury signature procedure in addition to a statement next to or beneath where the witness has to sign as follows: *'I confirm that I was physically present when [name of signatory] signed this deed'*.

Completion Information and Undertakings (2019) – Make it clear that a transfer signed in accordance with the Mercury procedure will be handed over (if agreed by both conveyancers) and vary the responses to 2.2 and 3.2(a) accordingly.

Code for Completion by Post (2019) – under para 13 (iii), the seller's solicitor undertakes to send the documents specified in para 9 to the buyer's solicitor; this includes the transfer. Any undertaking should be varied (preferably prior to exchange of contracts) to make it clear that a transfer signed in accordance with the Mercury procedure will be handed over (if agreed by both conveyancers).

As with any undertaking, the seller's conveyancer should carefully consider whether they are in a position to comply with it at the time that it is given and the undertaking should be amended accordingly.

Whether a conveyancing firm is willing to accept documents signed in this way is an assessment of risk for that particular firm.

When might Mercury signatures be used?

Note that, despite the fact that HMLR moved on very swiftly to announce that they would accept witnessed electronic signatures (now conveyancer-certified electronic signatures) on deeds, HMLR will still accept deeds signed using the Mercury signatures process. Examples of when a firm might use the Mercury signing process are:

- if their client is unable to attend the conveyancer's office to sign a deed at a face-to-face meeting. This is still very likely during a time of social distancing
- if their client is abroad and needs to sign a deed urgently (in the normal course of events, a conveyancer would anticipate this and arrange for a document to be returned by courier)
- if a firm does not have a conveyancer-certified electronic signature platform provider and for some reason is not able to secure their client's signature urgently to a document (e.g., due to travel restrictions, lockdown or postal delays)

Remember that if the process is going to be used, both conveyancers must agree to it and the client must have the facility to receive the document electronically, print it and scan or photograph the signature page and send it back to their conveyancer electronically.

CHAPTER FOUR

HMLR ACCEPTANCE OF ELECTRONIC SIGNATURES ON DEEDS – CONVEYANCER-CERTIFIED ELECTRONIC SIGNATURES

This chapter will consider why HMLR moved on from Mercury signatures so quickly along with the detail of HMLR's requirements set out in PG82 regarding the use of conveyancer-certified electronic signatures on deeds. This chapter will also highlight some of the practical issues and concerns which conveyancers should keep in mind when deciding whether to adopt the process and, if so, what questions to ask potential external suppliers of the required platform. This content was originally contained In PG8, but was moved to a newly created PG82 in March 2022.

HMLR permitted the use of Mercury signatures on deeds submitted for registration from 4 May 2020 as a response to the Covid-19 pandemic. It was perceived that this would assist conveyancers during lockdown when their clients could not leave their homes. However, HMLR received feedback that clients did not have printers or scanners in their homes enabling them to easily return the scanned signature page to their conveyancer which led to the fast move towards the acceptance of the 'witnessed electronic signature', as it was originally called. HMLR was looking at this form of signature before the pandemic, but Covid-19 sped things up. It is not clear how much call there was from the profession for HMLR to accept Mercury signatures or, indeed, to supplant them to a large extent with witnessed electronic signatures only three months later. Note, however, that under PG82, the 'witnessed electronic signature' is now called the 'conveyancer-certified electronic signature' and both this and Mercury signatures are now acceptable to HMLR.

Apart from the disadvantages above, Mercury signatures could be somewhat laborious to use. It is fair to say that conveyancers would need to give a very clear instructions to clients as to how to use them. Indeed, conveyancers may even deem it necessary to oversee the process via Skype, zoom or similar medium. This would involve the conveyancer spending time to ensure that the process is properly followed. Conveyancers are all too familiar with the difficulty of explaining the relatively straightforward process of adding a witnessed wet ink signature to a document in hardcopy, so the prospect of explaining the Mercury signing process to clients in an easy-to-follow format might be daunting.

A further risk associated with Mercury signatures is the fact that they rely on email both to send the document to be signed to the client, and for its return to the conveyancer. Few firms will have encrypted emails. Thus, attaching important documents to emails runs the usual cybercrime risk of interception by fraudsters. It is arguable that the conveyancer cannot be absolutely sure that the email received from the client has attached to it the document which the client has actually signed.

Thus, less than three months after agreeing to accept Mercury signatures, HMLR announced via a blog post that, from 27 July 2020, it would accept for registration documents which have been signed using the 'witnessed electronic signature' process.

Deeds that HMLR will accept that have been signed using the conveyancer-certified electronic signature

These are helpfully laid out by HMLR in a table in Appendix 1 of PG82, but some of the most common are:

- a deed that affects one of the dispositions in s 27 (2) and (3) LRA 2002 – these include:
    - A transfer
    - A lease of more than 7 years (that is, a lease registrable at HMLR in its own right)
    - A deed of easement

  - A legal charge (mortgage)

- a discharge or release in form DS1 or form DS3
- equivalent deeds in respect of unregistered land
- an assent of registered or unregistered land
- a power of attorney – but not a Lasting Power of Attorney
- a deed of substituted security in respect of registered land, incorporating a discharge or release and a grant of a new charge, that has been electronically signed in this way, even though the discharge or release will not be in form DS1 or form DS3, provided there is nothing to prevent the deed from being regarded as sufficient proof of satisfaction of the charge (rule 114 (4) of the Land Registration Rules 2003)

Remember the exception that Lasting Powers of Attorney must be signed using wet ink signatures.

A deed can be signed using the conveyancer-certified electronic signature procedure by an individual (or individuals) on their own behalf. Someone can also sign on behalf of another person (see comments below in 'HMLR requirements' regarding attorneys).

If a deed is being signed on behalf of a company by two 'authorised signatories' under s 44(2)(a) 2006 Act, HMLR points out that no witness will be involved and the requirements are to be 'read accordingly'.

Let's now consider the detail of HMLR's requirements set out in section 3.2 of PG82

HMLR requirements (© Crown copyright).	**Implications for conveyancers**
1. All the parties to the disposition or other dealing, including any parties who are not signing, are represented by a conveyancer. *The requirement for all the parties to be represented is subject to the following exceptions: only:* • *the lender in the case of a mortgage, discharge or release* • *the personal representatives in the case of an assent* • *the donor in the case of a power of attorney* *need have conveyancers acting for them.*	This means that in most conveyancing transactions where conveyancer-certified electronic signatures might be used, all parties have instructed a conveyancer.
	Note that if a firm adopts the process but acts, for example, on a transfer of equity or matrimonial matter where the other party is unrepresented, it will not be possible to use the conveyancer-certified electronic signature in that transaction.

Where a document is to be signed electronically by a party's attorney, a conveyancer must be acting in respect of the execution, but it does not matter for the purposes of these requirements whether the conveyancer was instructed by the party or by the attorney.	This makes it clear that deeds being signed by an attorney can use the conveyancer-certified electronic signature procedure. Remember that a Lasting Power of Attorney document cannot be signed using this process. Remember also that a conveyancer must obtain the identification documents of both the donor (party) and the attorney.
2. All the conveyancers involved agree to the use of conveyancer-certified electronic signatures. (Note that this does not mean that they must agree to all the signatures being in this form (see 'Mixed signing').)	Note that the 'conveyancers' must agree, not the parties. It is presumed that conveyancers will obtain their client's consent to using the process, particularly due to the steps outlined below that the client has to follow. A firm may wish to seek confirmation that the conveyancer on the other side of the transaction also has their client's consent. A firm cannot be forced to accept a document signed using a conveyancer-certified electronic signature.
3. A conveyancer is responsible for setting up and controlling the signing process through the platform.	As can be seen below, the conveyancer arranging for the document to be signed (typically, therefore, the seller's conveyancer) is involved at every stage of the signing process.

4. The signing and dating process is as follows.	
STEP 1 –The conveyancer controlling the signing process:	This is typically the seller's conveyancer.
uploads the final agreed copy of the document (including any plans) to the platform. To make clear what is expected (although this is not a requirement), conveyancers drafting the deed may wish to add a statement to the following effect next to or beneath where the witness is to sign: 'I confirm that I was physically present when [name of the party signing] signed this deed.'	It is important to ensure that both conveyancers have specifically confirmed their approval to the final version of the deed being signed using this process. In recent times practice has developed whereby the seller's conveyancer will arrange for their seller client to sign a form of transfer early in the transaction which has often not been formally approved by the buyer's conveyancer. See further Practice Points below. A significant risk to the conveyancer acting for the signatory in using this process is that the conveyancer has not fully explained the nature of the document being signed to the client. In the traditional process, the conveyancer will often send the transfer document to their seller client together with written explanation as to its meaning and significance. There is thus very little risk of the signatory claiming that they did not understand or intend to enter into the deed which, as we have seen, can lead to the deed being invalid.

	Thus, the seller's conveyancer should ensure that there is sufficient time during the transaction to agree the form of the transfer with the other side and report fully on it to their client in writing prior to setting up the signing process in the platform. Given the risk to the buyer's conveyancer and their client of a claim that the transfer could be invalid, the buyer's conveyancer may wish to obtain specific confirmation from the seller's conveyancer that the above steps have been carried out and further that the seller fully understands the nature of the document being signed.
populates the platform with the name, email address and mobile phone number of the signatories and the witnesses. Where the platform allows, the details for a witness can be populated later, either by the signatory entering the details for their witness or the conveyancer doing so, provided this is done before STEP 5	This requirement means that the seller's conveyancer will need to know *in advance* of the signing process the email address and phone number of all signatories (which they are likely to have on file) but also these details for all witnesses. This is a significant change in the process for the seller's conveyancer and will involve further information gathering earlier in the transaction. Note that all of the legal and 'best practice' requirements detailed in Chapter 2 regarding witnesses apply equally to the conveyancer-certified electronic signature process.

	From a risk management point of view, conveyancers should consider only completing the relevant fields on the platform when they have all required details for both the signatory and the witnesses. It is interesting that these instructions state 'where the platform allows' in relation to adding witness details later because these generic instructions recognise that different platform providers are developing their products in different ways. It is essential for a firm considering entering into a contract with a platform provider to ensure that all of the steps contained in these requirements can be specifically met.
highlights the fields that need completing within the document and indicates by whom they are to be completed, setting out the order (so the witness is after the signatory whose signing they are witnessing). In order to comply with STEP 6, a conveyancer must date the document in the platform. The controlling conveyancer may wish, therefore, to highlight the date field as one that requires completing in the signing flow and assign it to the conveyancer dating the document	Conveyancers will need to ensure that they have straightforward step-by-step instructions to inform signatories and witnesses how to use the platform and adopt the process. Again, it would make sense to ensure that the client signatory has been given this information well in advance of the actual signing date. It is essential that the witness and the signatory are present together and that the witness sees the signatory sign their name. This can be done through a window or car window, for example if social distancing requires it. However, the signatory and witness must be in each other's

	physical presence at the time of signing. This means that witnessing cannot take place via Skype, zoom or similar medium. The buyer's conveyancer may wish to add an additional provision in the transfer (clause 11 in the TR1 and clause 12 in the TP1) to the effect that the signing took place using an electronic signature platform and consider naming the platform provider. HMLR suggests adding a statement next to or beneath where the witnesses to sign to confirm that the witness and the signatory were together at the same time when the document was signed. HMLR suggests: *'I confirm that I was physically present when [name of signatory] signed this deed'* This highlights the importance of agreeing the form of transfer well in advance of the signing process.
STEP 2 – The platform emails the signatories to give them access to the document.	When sourcing a platform provider, conveyancers may wish to pay particular attention to this step. Using unencrypted email is a significant cybercrime risk because there is the risk of interception. A more secure form of email communication would be desirable.

STEP 3 – The platform texts the signatories an OTP, with a minimum of six numbers.	Conveyancers must ensure that the platform provider they use complies with this specific requirement namely the provision of a one-time password (OTP) of a minimum of six numbers. Not all electronic signature platforms on the market will be set up in this way but for the moment at least, this is a specific HMLR requirement which must be complied with. HMLR has suggested that this requirement may change over time. They may accept different methods of authentication in the future, such as a telephone call instead of a text.
STEP 4 – The signatories enter the OTP and sign the document in the physical presence of the witness, with the date and time being automatically recorded within the platform's audit trail.	There are two elements here. First the signatory and the witness must understand that the witness has to be in the presence of the signatory at the time of signing. Second the conveyancer must be satisfied that the platform provider has the appropriate audit trail which can be produced in an accessible, readable format to record the date and time that the signatory and witness signed the document. Note that in this context, 'signed' means adding an electronic signature within the platform.

STEP 5 – Once the signatory has signed the document, the witness will receive an email from the platform inviting them to sign and add their details in the space provided in the attestation clause. The witness inputs an OTP sent to them by text message by the platform, signs and adds their address in the space provided, with the date and time being automatically recorded again.	It is clear from this step that the conveyancer will need to know who the witness will be well in advance of embarking on the signing process. Clearly the witness will need a mobile phone in addition to the signatory to enable them to receive the appropriate email, one-time password text and to carry out the electronic signing. See above re possible future changes and further comments in Practice Points below.
STEP 6 – Once the signing process has been concluded, the conveyancer controlling the signing process dates the document within the platform with the date it took effect. *(There will be a gap between this step and the previous one if, as will often be the case, the deed is signed by all the signatories and witnesses some time in advance of completion.)*	This does not mean that the deed has to be dated on the day that the signing and witnessing was carried out. To ensure that the process runs smoothly and the buyer's conveyancer can carry out appropriate checks and safeguards to be satisfied that the deed has been signed properly (see Practice Points below), it is advisable to arrange for a transfer to be signed well before completion, possibly even before exchange. The wording in brackets acknowledges that the deed will often be signed in readiness for completion, in advance of the completion date.

	Note that the 'conveyancer controlling the process' dates the deed. This suggests that only one conveyancer on the file should deal with the signing process and dating of the deed (which will be the date of completion of a transfer). Note that HMLR has changed its terminology from the previous version to refer to signing the 'document' rather than 'deed'; but here, reference to 'deed' remains in the wording in brackets re the signature gap.
STEP 7 – The conveyancer who lodges the application does so by electronic means and includes with the application: • *a PDF of the completed document. Where the application is for first registration, a print-out of the PDF, certified to be a true copy of the original deed, can be lodged* • *a certificate (not necessarily signed by them: see below) in the following form: 'I certify that, to the best of my knowledge and belief, the applicable requirements set out in practice guide 82 for the use of conveyancer-certified electronic signatures have*	This requirement now switches to the buyer's conveyancer (as they will be submitting the HMLR application in a purchase transaction). Note that for a registered title, it is not possible to send a deed signed using this process as a paper application to HMLR. Note the wording of the certification: 'certified to be a true copy of the original deed' This is a certification which must accompany the application for registration and is probably the most controversial part of the process because it requires a conveyancer to certify in their own name that HMLR's requirements have been complied with.

been satisfied.' The certificate needs to be dated and signed by an individual conveyancer, their full name and firm or employer must be added and the deed or deeds for which the certificate is given must be specified. Appendix 2 contains an example of an acceptable certificate	Note that the certificate can be given by the buyer's conveyancer or the seller's conveyancer (see further below).
This certificate will be read by HM Land Registry as referring to the requirements as they were on the relevant date. This means that if, for example, the requirements in respect of the signing process change but the signing process has been completed before the date on which the requirements changed, the certificate will be read as referring to those particular requirements as they were before the change.	Note that HMLR states that the certificate is confirming the requirements 'as they were on the relevant date'. They acknowledge that their signing requirements might change between the date the document was signed and completion. In this case, the certificate is confirming that the requirements at the date of signing were met, so it will not be necessary to get the document re-signed to comply with any intervening changes. This seems to accept that the HMLR process and/or requirements may change over time and, fairly quickly. Thus, it is very important for conveyancers to ensure that they keep a dated record of the HMLR requirements that were in force at the date of signing in case HMLR practice changes between that date and the application for registration.

	HMLR has indicated that they will keep records of the changes but a prudent conveyancer will no doubt wish to retain that evidence on their own file. See comments below on Appendix 2 and further Practice Points.
The certificate can be given by any party's conveyancer who has satisfied themselves that the deed has been duly executed. In most cases involving transfers, the conveyancer controlling the signing process will be the seller's conveyancer and the conveyancer lodging the application will be the buyer's conveyancer. The certificate might then be signed by the seller's conveyancer and passed on to the buyer's conveyancer; alternatively, the buyer's conveyancer, having been satisfied on completion that the deed was duly executed, might sign the certificate, bearing in mind its qualified terms. *A conveyancer is not precluded from giving the certificate because they have signed the deed themselves on behalf of a party, acting under a power of attorney.*	This means that HMLR will accept a certificate on registration signed by the buyer's conveyancer or the seller's conveyancer. This will represent a risk that firms will have to assess. See further comments below.

The registrar will rely on the conveyancer's certificate lodged with the application. Any audit report or certificate of completion issued by the platform must not be lodged with the application but should be retained. It may contain personal data and would be open to public inspection.	Note the reliance by HMLR on the certificate. This has implications which both firms must consider. A seller's conveyancer may wish to obtain an undertaking from a buyer's conveyancer that the audit report will not be sent to HMLR with the registration as it might contain their client's personal details. But what if HMLR raises a requisition as to execution? It might be necessary for the buyer's conveyancer to submit the audit report to HMLR to respond to such a requisition. They would need to obtain the consent of the seller's conveyancer to do so, which might be difficult post completion.
	It is suggested that conveyancers will need to change their terms and conditions to accommodate the above requirements, obtain email and mobile phone numbers for witnesses and signatories early in the transaction and, to avoid last-minute concerns, both conveyancers should consider arranging for the signing process to be carried out prior to exchange of contracts. See Practice Points below for further comment

The conveyancer's certificate

A key element of the conveyancer-certified electronic signature procedure is the certificate to be given to HMLR by the buyer's conveyancer when submitting a deed for registration that has been signed using this procedure.

HMLR has produced a suggested form of certificate in PG82 Appendix 2 (Acceptable certificate for conveyancer-certified electronic signatures) as follows:

> *To HM Land Registry*
>
> *Title Number: AB1234*
>
> *Property Description: The freehold/leasehold land shown edged with red on the plan of the above title and being [property address]*
>
> *Proprietor/Applicant:*
>
> *Deed/document for which this certificate is given:*
>
> *I act for the Proprietor/Applicant.*
>
> *I certify that, to the best of my knowledge and belief, the requirements set out in practice guide 82 for the use of conveyancer-certified electronic signatures have been satisfied.*
>
> *Signature of individual conveyancer:*
>
> *Full name of individual conveyancer:*
>
> *Name of individual conveyancer's firm:*
>
> *Address of firm:*
>
> *Date of this certificate:*
>
>

One of the most important things to note here is that the certificate is to be given in the name of the individual conveyancer, not the firm. It raises different issues depending on whether it is given by the seller's conveyancer or buyer's.

Seller's conveyancer

The option for the seller's conveyancer to give the certificate confirming compliance with PG82 is one of HMLR's most significant changes to the process. On the one hand, a certificate signed by the seller's conveyancer makes sense because they have control over the platform, so it might be appropriate for them to give the certificate. However, conveyancers must consider whether they will be willing to give a certificate which involves them in the buyer's registration application. They might effectively be doing this in any event because a prudent conveyancer acting for a buyer is likely to seek confirmation from the seller's conveyancer that their platform and the signing process will comply with the requirements in PG82. However, it feels like quite a significant step for HMLR to accept a certification from the seller's conveyancer in relation to an application submitted by another firm. This does create a direct relationship between the seller's conveyancer and HMLR that has not existed before.

Buyer's conveyancer

Conveyancing firms which have specific post completion departments will need to consider their procedures. The requirement to give a named certificate will mean that the fee earner with conduct of the purchase must complete the certificate to pass to the post completion team to submit with the application for registration. In so doing, the buyer's conveyancer is certifying that the seller's conveyancer has, via their platform, complied with the requirements of PG82.

The fact that the buyer's conveyancer is giving a personal certificate that the seller's conveyancer has complied with PG82 may result in a prudent buyer's conveyancer obtaining an undertaking from the seller's conveyancer prior to completion to confirm that the seller's conveyancer will meet the requirements of PG82.

HMLR recognises that this is a concern to conveyancers.

PG82 contains specific requirements that must be met for Mercury signing and conveyancer-certified electronic signatures where the dealing is by a company. Conveyancers should note that HMLR casts some doubt here: *'We think that there must be doubt as to whether a company can use some form of electronic common seal as section 45 of the Companies Act 2006 appears to envisage a physical seal. We also think there must be some uncertainty at the moment as to whether one authorised signatory can sign using one type of signature and the other using another.'*

What documents can be signed using these procedures?

One of the most helpful Inclusions to PG82 is Appendix 1 which contains a list of documents and forms and indicates whether they can be signed using the Mercury signing process, the conveyancer-certified electronic signature or 'other' electronic signature. Conveyancers should check this list every time they consider having a document signed in any way other than traditional wet Ink.

Practice Points

There are a lot of practice points arising from the new procedure which conveyancing teams should consider if they decide to adopt the conveyancer-certified electronic signature process. The process will impact on the timing of certain tasks (e.g., agreeing the form of the transfer and arranging for signature), reporting to clients (e.g., as to the effect of the document/s being signed using the platform) and ensuring that clear and comprehensive explanation has been sent to clients who will be using the platform. It is imperative for both conveyancers to ensure that the validity of a deed cannot subsequently be challenged on the grounds of inadequate signing or witnessing procedures.

Conveyancers agreement to use the platform

Both conveyancers must agree to use the platform. Conveyancers should consider raising the following question on every purchase:

Are you proposing to use a platform provider for conveyancer-certified electronic signatures for signing the transfer?

If the seller's conveyancer replies in the affirmative, the buyer's conveyancer can object if they do not agree and seek specific confirmation that the transfer will be signed and witnessed using wet ink signatures. This is imperative for the buyer's conveyancer. They must avoid the situation where they have paid away the completion money thinking that they will receive a transfer signed using wet ink signatures but, in fact, receive one signed using conveyancer-certified electronic signatures. Whilst the buyer's conveyancer would be entitled to demand a further transfer, this is of little comfort if the completion money has been paid over.

We have noted in chapter 2 the inclination of some conveyancing firms to email scanned contracts post exchange, despite this being in breach of undertaking. This is effectively presenting the other conveyancer with an intractable fait accompli. It is reasonable to assume that some firms might try to adopt a similar practice in relation to conveyancer-certified electronic signatures on deeds, leases and transfers. It has been reported that some seller's conveyancers have tried to force the buyer's conveyancer to accept documents signed using conveyancer-certified electronic signatures post completion. The fact that this is not acceptable under the Code for Completion by Post (2019) or PG82 will be of little comfort to buyer's conveyancer if they are struggling to obtain a wet ink signed transfer with their priority period expiry looming.

If the buyer's conveyancer is prepared in principle to proceed using conveyancer-certified electronic signatures, this will probably give rise to additional points to be agreed between the conveyancers such as:

- which platform provider is being used?
- security of the platform
- confirmation that the platform is fully compliant with HMLR's requirements in PG82

Audit report

In PG82, HMLR 'advises' firms to retain with their conveyancing file a copy of the completion certificate or audit report produced by the electronic signature platform at the end of the signing process. Note firstly therefore that this is not one of HMLR's specific requirements that *must* be met but is essential evidence from the point of view of the buyer's conveyancer as to the signing and witnessing process within the platform.

The certificate or report should give an audit trail of the signing including:

- the time and date of the signatures
- email addresses the document was sent to
- the one-time password method used
- the fields that were completed, and
- the IP addresses of the devices that were used

The above is all recommended by HMLR. It should be straightforward for the platform providers to capture this information but the conveyancers will both need to be satisfied that the information can be made available in a straightforward, downloadable, readable format.

The audit report also contains significant personal details about people who are not clients of the firm, for example the witnesses. Any firm subscribing with a platform provider should ensure that all regulatory, GDPR and confidentiality issues are addressed regarding data capture and storage, bearing in mind that this detail will need to be provided to the buyer's conveyancer when acting for the seller.

The seller's conveyancer should obtain the written authority of their seller client and all witnesses to supply the audit report containing the above information to the buyer's conveyancer. As we have seen above, it may also be necessary to send the audit report to HMLR if they raise a requisition as to the signing and witnessing process.

Agreeing the form of transfer

The form of transfer (or deed being signed using the platform) should be agreed at the earliest possible point in the transaction. This is likely to be reasonably straightforward on a transfer of whole, but a transfer of part often involves a number of amendments, many of them made at the last minute.

CQS accredited firms must follow the Protocol

Paragraph 13 (pre-exchange) suggests that the seller's conveyancer 'considers' including a draft transfer when they draft the contract and send the contract package to the buyer's conveyancer. Given the importance to the buyer's conveyancer of ensuring that the transfer contains additional provisions (see above as to presence of witness), the buyer's conveyancer should react if they receive a draft transfer from the seller's conveyancer and, preferably, append the agreed form of transfer to the contract if the conveyancer-certified electronic signature process is going to be used.

Paragraph 19 (pre-exchange) suggests that the buyer's conveyancer approves the draft contract and send the draft transfer deed and Completion Information and Undertakings form (TA13) to the seller's conveyancer. It would be prudent to do this rather than agree the form of transfer after exchange of contracts and before completion.

Paragraph 24 (post exchange) requires the seller's conveyancer to provide a copy of the transfer executed by the seller, to be delivered on completion. Upon receipt of the of the transfer, the buyer's conveyancer should check execution of the copy transfer supplied and consider whether the transfer requires execution by the buyer.

This part of the process at paragraph 24 is very important for the buyer's conveyancer. To ensure that this happens, the buyer's conveyancer should ask the following early in the transaction:

'Please confirm that, prior to completion and in accordance with the Law Society Conveyancing Protocol, a copy of the signed (but undated) transfer will be supplied to us and on completion you will also supply the [platform

provider] audit report to enable us to check the signing and witnessing procedures.

Any suggestion that this is an 'indiscriminate enquiry' and should not be answered must be resisted by the buyer's conveyancer for the same reasons as outlined below.

The buyer's conveyancer could raise the following additional points:

> *'Please confirm by way of undertaking that you will:*
>
> *a) ensure that the conveyancer providing the HMLR certificate will attend to dating the transfer with the date of completion pursuant to step six of HMLR's requirements set out in section 2.3 of HMLR Practice Guide 82*
>
> *b) provide on completion the transfer duly signed and dated within the [insert platform provider name] platform along with the audit report[s] evidencing all events of signing and dating*
>
> *c) deal immediately and at your client's expense with any requisition/s which HMLR raises in relation to the transfer (and certificate if required) and, if required, confirm that you will provide a further signed, witnessed and dated transfer in the event that HMLR rejects the transfer provided on completion for any reason or cancels the application for registration*
>
> *d) on completion, will retain a certified copy of the transfer supplied on completion (or a copy within the [insert name of platform provider] platform)'*

It is fair to say that a seller's conveyancer might resist giving undertakings in the above form, but they are all issues upon which the conveyancers will need to reach agreement.

Do any questions between conveyancers about conveyancer certified electronic signatures amount to 'enquiries'?

The buyer's conveyancer should not include any questions as above with the additional enquiries on a purchase because the seller's conveyancer may refuse to answer on the basis that they are indiscriminate 'standard additional enquiries' which are prohibited for CQS accredited firms by the Protocol. The Protocol directs buyers' conveyancers to:

> *'Raise only specific additional enquiries required to clarify issues arising out of the documents submitted, or which are relevant to the title, existing or planned use, nature or location of the property or which the buyer has expressly requested.'* [© Law Society. Protocol, buyer, pre-exchange, para 15].

Any pre-contract questions relating to the method of signature of the transfer, the platform provider, process or certificate relate directly to matters of title and are thus inherent to the conveyancing process. Such questions would not be standard additional enquiries. If the seller's conveyancer refuses to provide this information, the buyer's conveyancer should not proceed to exchange until such time as the method for signing the transfer is clear and agreed.

Undertakings regarding the transfer

As with the Mercury signed transfer, consider the implied undertakings and amend accordingly.

Completion Information and Undertakings (2019) – Make it clear that a transfer signed in accordance with the conveyancer-certified electronic signature procedure will be handed over (if agreed by both conveyancers) and vary the responses to 2.2 and 3.2(a) accordingly.

Code for Completion by Post (2019) – under para 13 (iii), the seller's solicitor undertakes to send the documents specified in para 9 to the buyer's solicitor; this includes the transfer. Any undertaking should be varied (preferably prior to exchange of contracts) to make it clear that a transfer signed in accordance with the conveyancer-certified electronic signature procedure will be handed over (if agreed by both conveyancers). Further, the buyer's conveyancer should consider whether they want to send the seller's conveyancer instructions under para 9 of the Code, to make it clear that they expect to receive a hard copy of an original, dated transfer on completion rather than merely a scanned copy sent by email. The seller's conveyancer should be mindful of the above undertaking.

As with any undertaking, the seller's conveyancer should carefully consider whether they are in a position to comply with it at the time that it is given and the undertaking should be amended accordingly.

Considerations relating to using the platform

Remember that many of the issues relating to the integrity of the system and the process are of equal concern to conveyancers acting for both seller and buyer. Either conveyancer must give a certificate to be submitted to HMLR on registration confirming that the requirements of PG82 have been met. Conveyancers will need to agree who is going to give this certificate. Logic demands that the seller's conveyancer gives the certificate as they have control over the signing platform and process, but, as we have seen, this does directly involve the seller's conveyancer in the buyer's registration. HMLR will '*rely on the conveyancer's certificate lodged with the application*'.

The likely outcome of this compulsory certificate is that the buyer's conveyancer will seek very specific confirmation and/or warranties from the seller's conveyancer that the requirements have been met.

Certificate must be given in the name of a conveyancer

Whether the certificate is given by the seller's conveyancer or the buyer's, HMLR is clear that it must be given in the name of the individual conveyancer and not that of their firm. HMLR says that this reflects the importance of the certificate that they will be relying on. Some individual conveyancers may be reluctant to sign in their own name – it is not clear whether HMLR is seeking to impose personal liability on the individual. This does not seem logical because the application for registration is being given by a firm (the vast majority of which will use the portal and have the appropriate agreement in place with HMLR) and it is the firm which will have indemnity insurance in place in the event that something goes wrong.

Firms should consider what happens if the conveyancer who has control of the signing process leaves the firm, or is absent when the HMLR certificate must be issued. This would necessitate another conveyancer in the firm giving the certificate, but they would have to satisfy themselves that the signing process had been followed.

How does the conveyancer (whether acting for seller or buyer) know that the witness and the signatory are together?

Of course, this question is just as relevant to a signature process using a wet ink signature but is likely to be raised because the conveyancer-certified electronic signatures process is new and will prompt more scrutiny.

The seller's conveyancer could conduct the signing process by Skype, zoom (or other similar process). Note that the conveyancer would not be the witness in this instance as they would not be 'present' – the purpose is just to oversee the signing and witnessing. In this instance it would be possible to record the event but the firm would have to deal with storage and data protection issues. A more straightforward solution would be for the seller's conveyancer to make a contemporaneous attendance note detailing the process of signing, persons involved, order of signing etc.

As indicated above, it would be prudent for the buyer's conveyancer to amend the transfer to make it clear on the face of the document that the seller and the witness were together at the time of the electronic signing. It may be apparent from the provider's audit report if there is a gap in time between the two signatures being created.

The requirement to issue a one-time password to the witness and the fact that this has to go to another device, would suggest that a different person is involved which should give the conveyancers sufficient reassurance that there is a witness in place.

Arranging for signature

Any new process will be more time consuming to start with. The seller's conveyancer will have to send clear, specific instructions to their seller client to ensure that the process is followed correctly. Conveyancers will be all too aware of the fact that often clients seem unable to follow the simplest instructions regarding signing documents and many will therefore have little faith that following a procedure involving conveyancer-certified electronic signatures will be any more successful.

What will the signatures look like?

This will depend on the platform provider. Some signatures will no doubt appear electronically but as a 'signature' whereby the person signing uses their finger or a stylus to sign their name. In other cases, the signature may simply be a code or a printed or typed name to indicate that the document has been signed. It is possible that a transfer using conveyancer-certified electronic signatures might be indistinguishable from one using a wet ink signature. There may be codes showing the date and time of signature on the transfer itself. If not, this should be recorded on the audit report which the buyer's conveyancer should insist on receiving, preferably by way of undertaking.

Risks of online signing

One of the benefits of sending a hardcopy of a transfer for a wet signature is that a letter explaining the purpose of the transfer (or other deed) can be sent in advance which gives the signatory time to read and digest the advice in the letter. A signatory could argue that they did not appreciate the significance or importance of the document that they were signing if this is done electronically on a mobile device. They might not read a document on a small screen or turn their mind to the importance of the document that they are signing.

Some platform providers may require that signatories actually sign their name or include their mark electronically within the platform to indicate that the signatory appreciates they are signing an important document. The platform providers may also include a receipt or acknowledgement confirming that the signatory has read and understood the nature of the document that they are signing. This receipt would be sent electronically to the signatories' conveyancer and would act as a further safeguard against a claim that a client did not understand the nature of what they were signing.

These issues are human weaknesses rather than legal ones but go to the heart of the document signing process. If a signatory claims that they did not understand what they were signing or agree to its contents, it could be invalid.

Whatever the process, it is important for both conveyancers to be sure that the signatories understand the importance of the documents being signed. This is important for conveyancers because they are the only parties who are properly insured in the conveyancing process and thus are at risk in the event of a party not understanding the significance of signing a particular document electronically.

Dating the transfer

It is not necessary for the conveyancer-certified electronic signatures to be added to the transfer on the day of completion. Indeed, this would probably represent a time-consuming risk both for seller and buyer's conveyancer and the seller client is unlikely to want to be dealing with the signature of the transfer, whether electronic or otherwise, on the day of completion itself.

Thus, the transfer should, ideally, be signed and witnessed electronically before the completion date. The seller's conveyancer must insert the completion date within the platform on the day of completion. The audit report should also record this part of the process.

Costs

Conveyancing firms will need to consider whether any additional time spent dealing with conveyancer-certified electronic signatures should be charged for. This is a decision for each individual firm. Most firms would probably absorb the cost of any additional time (particularly if early adopters of the process) and might weigh this against the money saved in not having to send a paper copy of the transfer by post.

If a firm decides to make any changes to its cost structure as a result of adopting the process, they should make any consequential changes to the costs schedule on their website (pursuant to the Transparency Rules).

How many people in a conveyancing firm/team will be authorised to use the conveyancer-certified electronic signature process?

This links to the fact that the conveyancer must give the required certificate to confirm compliance with PG82 in their own name and not that of the firm. From a risk management point of view, a firm may decide to limit the number of conveyancers who are authorised to use the process to ensure that proper training is given by the platform provider, sensible amendments to precedents and letters can be made etc.

It is fair to say that conveyancer-certified electronic signatures are likely to be embraced by the conveyancing industry as a whole on a piecemeal basis. Thus, those firms which adopt the process are not likely to encounter its use very often, at least initially. Tasks which are not carried out regularly represent a risk to the firm. Thus, limiting the conveyancers within a team who are authorised to use the process to named individuals would be an effective way of managing this risk.

Those firms which have separate post completion teams should remember to make the necessary adjustments to their processes to ensure that the conveyancer's certificate accompanies the transfer and HMLR application when submitted.

What about the lenders?

If a conveyancing firm embraces the conveyancer-certified electronic signature process, they may wish to expand its use into the signature of the mortgage deed. However, they should not do this without specific written authority from the lender in question.

The UK Finance Handbook requires conveyancers to:

- If supplied by the lender, give the mortgage conditions to borrower/s before completion of the mortgage (para 11.1.1), and
- Explain the responsibilities and liabilities to each borrower (or other signatory) (para 11.1.2), and
- Ensure that the required signature/s are witnessed by an independent person who must sign their name and add their name and address in legible form (para 11.2.1), and

- Ensure that all documents are be dated with the completion date of the loan (para 11.2.1).

There is nothing else in the Handbook about signatures and the lenders have not made a formal announcement as to whether they will accept conveyancer-certified electronic signatures to mortgage deeds. An article in the Mortgage Finance Gazette of 21.05.2020 points out that it was reported in 2019 that indemnity claims for property fraud and error cost HMLR in excess of £70 million over 14 years. The article was written after 4 May 2020 when HMLR indicated its acceptance of the Mercury signature procedure but before the announcement on 27 July 2020 that 'witnessed' electronic signatures to deeds would be accepted.

The article takes the view that the Mercury signing approach does not change the law for signature of mortgage deeds and further that mortgage deeds should be signed using the traditional wet signature and witnessing process.

No lenders have any additional Part 2 amendments to para 11 of the Handbook above. This is perhaps because the lenders consider that the requirements regarding the signature of the mortgage deed are straightforward and uncontroversial.

It is not clear whether lenders are prepared to agree to mortgage deeds being signed using the conveyancer-certified electronic signature procedure. If conveyancers decide to adopt the process, they should contact each lender directly for their instructions. Some lenders may (as is commonly the case) simply pass the responsibility for ensuring that the mortgage deed is properly signed and witnessed back to the conveyancer.

However, note that we are talking about a mortgage deed which creates contractual liabilities between the lender and the buyer/borrower. This means that the mortgage deed is not simply a document which is used for registration (unlike the transfer of whole in many cases), but is a document which the lender might seek to rely on for the full term of the loan. Thus, the signing and witnessing to ensure validity of this deed is of long-term and material significance to the conveyancer acting for the lender. If the lender has not authorised using conveyancer-certified electronic signatures, the conveyancer must continue to attend to signing and witnessing using wet ink signatures on the mortgage deed. The fact that HMLR is willing to accept a mortgage deed signed electronically does not mean that this process is automatically acceptable to the lenders.

Note from para 11 of the Handbook above that the conveyancer should read the instructions in the mortgage offer in every case to establish the particular witnessing requirements. Some lenders specify that the mortgage deed should only be witnessed by a qualified person (typically a solicitor, licensed conveyancer or qualified legal executive). Some firms may consider that good risk management demands that the mortgage deed is witnessed in this way.

This must not be confused with the electronic process which some lenders have adopted on volume remortgage transactions. In this instance lenders have embraced e-signing (see chapter 3).

Buyer signing the transfer

In many cases, the buyer must sign the transfer; either because it contains an indemnity covenant and/or to affirm a co-ownership declaration between the buyers. There are various ways this could be done.

The seller's conveyancer could arrange (via the buyer's conveyancer) for the buyer to sign the transfer through the platform controlled by the seller's conveyancer. This would have the advantage of ensuring that all parties have signed the same document, but it would mean the buyer's contact details etc being made available to the seller's conveyancer to enable steps 1 to 5 of HMLR's signing process to take place. This raises the usual confidentiality issues.

Alternatively, the buyer's conveyancer could arrange for the buyer to sign a duplicate transfer via mixed signing.

Mixed signing

Section 4 of PG82 makes it clear that if it is necessary for one party to a deed to sign in wet ink (either in the usual way or via the Mercury signing process), and another to sign with an electronic signature, this can be done by way of counterpart deeds. The detail is contained in PG82.

It is also acceptable for parties to sign counterpart deeds each using a different electronic signature platform provided that the PG82 requirements are followed.

HMLR state that *'mixed signing in the sense of a signatory signing in wet ink and their witness signing with a conveyancer-certified electronic signature, and vice versa, is not acceptable. The requirements for conveyancer-certified electronic signatures involve a signatory and their witness both signing in the same way through the platform.'*

In all cases where an electronic signature platform is used, remember that the conveyancers must consent to its use. This is particularly important where a seller's conveyancer arranges for their client to sign one part of a deed electronically and the buyer's conveyancer arranges for their client to sign the counterpart using the traditional wet ink signature. This situation is likely to arise on a sale of a new build property by a developer where it is often the case that counterpart leases and transfers will be signed. The buyer's conveyancer should read the developer's contract for sale very carefully in this instance. Often the contract will require the buyer to sign a counterpart and hand it over on completion.

It is fair to say that a larger firm of conveyancers that carries out a lot of development work is more likely to adopt the conveyancer-certified electronic signatures procedure via a platform provider. A buyer's conveyancer is not obliged to accept a transfer signed in this way.

What about signing plans attached to deeds?

If the transfer of part or other deed includes a plan, it must be signed by the transferor or other disponor (rule 213(2) LRR 2003). Step 1 of the HMLR requirements set out in section 3.2 of PG82 states that the conveyancer controlling the signing process must upload the final agreed copy of the deed including any plans to the platform. Conveyancers must ensure that the platform enables an electronic signature to be added to any plans attached to a deed. The conveyancer could sign the plan on their client's behalf within the platform. Whether acting for seller or buyer, both conveyancers should be satisfied that the appropriate authority was given if the conveyancer signs a plan on their client's behalf.

When receiving a signed (but undated) transfer or document prior to completion to check that it has been properly signed and witnessed, the buyer's conveyancer must ensure that any plan attached has also been signed otherwise they will run the risk of a requisition from HMLR or a rejection of the application.

Amending a deed

A deed requiring registration may need to be changed due to a clerical or other error, or the parties may later decide that it does not sufficiently achieve their original intentions. PG68 explains how parties seeking to amend the effect of the deed intended to achieve a registrable disposition should proceed.

In relation to deeds signed using conveyancer-certified electronic signatures, practitioners should refer to section 3.3 of PG82. HMLR has issued 'interim guidance' on the issue pending a review. One option is to printout the executed deed and amend the printout adding the words: 'The electronic deed of which this is a printout is amended this day [date] as follows:...'

HMLR draws the distinction between whether an amendment is 'material' or not. If a party has not consented to a material amendment it is unenforceable as against that party. In the case of a non-material amendment, the endorsed printout need only be amended by an individual conveyancer acting for one of the parties, adding their signature and confirmation that they have their client's authority to do so. HMLR suggests that if there is any doubt as to whether the amendment is 'material', conveyancers will have the amendment countersigned by the parties to the deed.

The rest of this section details how the amended printout should be submitted to HMLR. A further alternative is to execute a deed of rectification or variation.

If it proves necessary to completely re-sign a document that had initially gone through the platform signing procedure, prudent conveyancers should check whether it is necessary for the subsequent document to be signed using the certified-conveyancer electronic signature process or whether a conventionally executed deed is acceptable if this is what all parties want.

Statements of truth (PG73)

HMLR has changed its procedure regarding signatures of statements of truth. Originally, the position was that they must be signed using a wet ink signature in the usual way. However, section 3.4 of PG82 confirms that HMLR can accept a statement of truth which has been signed using a conveyancer-certified electronic signature provided that the requirements set out in this section are met. They broadly follow the requirements for signing a deed referred to above but without the requirement for the signature to be witnessed.

The broader details regarding statements of truth are contained in PG73.

Platform providers

Conveyancers will need to research the market to establish which property technology ('prop tech') providers offer a conveyancer-certified electronic signature platform which meets HMLR's requirements set out in PG82. HMLR has made no secret of the fact that it is liaising and consulting with a number of providers regarding the development of the technology and indeed suggests that there are around 30 organisations engaging with them. However, there are far fewer providers in the market at the moment that will have the fully developed technology to offer a conveyancer-certified electronic signatures platform.

HMLR has been asked if it can supply a list of interested providers. Apparently, HMLR is considering this but will undoubtedly tread carefully because a government department cannot be seen to endorse any particular platform, product or provider. HMLR maybe developing some guidance for conveyancers in this area. Accordingly, conveyancers who are interested should subscribe to HMLR's regular updates.

Issues when choosing a platform provider

Conveyancers should spend the same degree of time, effort and due diligence in researching a suitable platform provider as they would when considering introducing a new case management system. They may wish to take the following issues into account when deciding which platform provider to use:

- One of the challenges for platform providers is that they may not be offering a solution or product which was specifically designed to fit in with the conveyancing process. This is because a number of providers already have the facility to offer electronic signatures which can be used for contracts and a range of other documents but which are not used for deeds. Thus, the providers are not necessarily set up to allow for witnessing as is required for a deed. A number of systems treat the witness as another party to the deed. Conveyancers should therefore request very specific demonstrations of the precise workings of the platforms.

- Conveyancers should also be permitted to 'try before they buy' and be allowed to work within a dummy version of the platform to ensure that it works effectively

- Those conveyancers who will be authorised to use the platform (and provide the required HMLR certificate) should be involved in the demonstrations, tests and training

- As with any IT product, conveyancers should establish what technical support and troubleshooting support is available. If the providers technical support will only be available between 9-to-5 Monday to Friday, conveyancers should ensure that they only send documents to their clients to sign and witness during these hours

- Conveyancers should also establish what happens within the system if the client manages to sign the document incorrectly or in some way fails to adopt the correct procedure. Such errors could mean that there are multiple versions of the same document within the platform. Conveyancers must understand how version control within the system works and how errors are handled. A knock-on for the buyer's conveyancer is to ensure that the correct audit report detailing the correct timings and procedures accompanies the final version of the transfer

- How will the one-time password requirement work in practice?
- How does the two-factor authentication work?
- Cost – is it a flat fee, monthly fee, cost per document or a combination of these?
- Firms should seek reassurance regarding security/hacking/frauds of the platform; this is central to a firm's risk management and should be the central focus of any discussion with a platform provider
- Obtain specific confirmation that the platform complies with HMLR's detailed requirements in PG82
- Does the process rely on unencrypted email which is weak from a cybercrime point of view?
- How does the platform provider propose storing the documents and data captured by the conveyancer-certified electronic signature process? E.g., in the cloud?
- How will the conveyancing firm gain access to the data?
- How does the conveyancer know that the correct people are signing the document?
- Ease-of-use/adoption
- The system must be able to track the profiles of individual signers and keep the data secure
- Choose a provider who explains the system in a way that the conveyancer can understand
- The seller's conveyancer must be able to give reassurance to the buyer's conveyancer as to the validity of the process – and

possibly be expected to give undertakings in this regard (and/or the certificate in Appendix 2 of PG82)

- Client journey/ease-of-use
- Is it something that the firm would want to invest in?
- Does it provide a better experience from the client?
- Is the system future proof? Given HMLR's comments regarding qualified electronic signatures, any system adopted now should not be quickly redundant
- If HMLR requirements move on, will the platform provider require further payment from the conveyancing firm to upgrade, amend or alter the platform?
- Does the platform provider have any form of insurance in place to indemnify the firm in the event that the system is hacked and client data compromised or fraud perpetrated?
- How long has the platform provider been in business?
- Firms should remember that they are obliged to retain client files for between 6 to 12 years – how can the platform provider reassure the firm that the data will be available in an accessible format for the required period of time?
- Conveyancing firms may wish to consider the audited accounts of the platform provider to establish the likely longevity of the provider. The requirements imposed on conveyancing firms regarding the retention of data from a regulatory and lender perspective is such that firms would want reassurance. There are a number of new entrants and start-up firms in this market
- Conveyancing firms should consider how they can access the data and audit trails if the platform provider goes out of business or merges with another organisation – conveyancers should not be

left in a position where they must make significant additional payments to obtain this data

- Conveyancing firms should consider receiving monthly updates of data from their platform provider in a format that the firm can securely store and access. In this event the firm should, of course, remember its own obligations in terms of data storage

- In more general terms, firms should keep their own IT systems up-to-date and replace software there is no longer supported

- Firms need to consider how a platform provider will integrate with the firm's own system particularly in relation to having multiple secure backups of data in place

Unfortunately, law firms often do not understand technology/process properly. Firms should involve their IT department/provider but the conveyancers and heads of department must be involved as well.

Conveyancers may be wary of using the process if they do not know what to expect. Thus, the seller's conveyancer should consider being proactive and showing the buyer's conveyancer a sample document indicating the format of the signatures, witnessing and dating etc to ensure that the buyer's conveyancer knows what to expect on completion. Anything which might demystify the process and encourage its use would benefit those firms which decide to adopt the process.

CHAPYER FIVE

RELEVANT CASE LAW

In this chapter some recent cases of particular relevance to conveyancers will be considered which are connected with some of the issues relating to electronic signatures and witnessing or the reliance which HMLR will place on conveyancers when making an application for registration.

Chief Land Registrar v Caffrey & Co [2016] EWCH 161 (Ch)

In this case, the High Court considered a claim regarding the submission to HMLR of a fraudulent DS1.

Summary of facts

The defendant was a firm of solicitors retained by Mr & Mrs Turner to act for them in the discharge of a mortgage over their registered property in favour of a bank, DB UK Bank Ltd. The bank was a victim of a fraud and the mortgage, which should not have been discharged, was removed by HMLR pursuant to the DS1 submitted by the defendant. The bank was indemnified by HMLR under the statutory scheme in the LRA 2002. By statute, HMLR thereby became entitled to exercise any cause of action which the bank could have exercised if the indemnity had not been paid. HMLR claimed that if no indemnity had been paid, the bank would have been entitled to pursue an action in negligence against the defendant arising out of the defendant's failure to verify facts and matters where it had assumed a duty to the bank to do so. In addition, HMLR claimed that it was entitled to bring in its own right a claim for misrepresentation made by the defendant in submitting documents to HMLR.

Detailed facts

Mr & Mrs Turner were registered proprietors of a property which they charged to the bank as security for a loan in 2007. Subsequently they instructed the defendant to act for them to arrange the discharge of the mortgage. They gave the defendant a form DS1 purportedly signed on behalf of the bank to discharge the mortgage. However, the DS1 was fraudulently signed. Mr & Mrs Turner told the defendant that the bank was represented by another firm of solicitors but this was also untrue. Somewhat surprisingly, the defendant failed to contact the bank or the solicitors allegedly instructed by them to verify the instructions. In other words, the defendant took no steps to verify the information handed to them and took their clients assertions and documents at face value.

To compound the issue, the defendant then submitted the form DS1 to HMLR together with a form AP1 to apply to alter the register and delete the charge. HMLR raised a requisition requesting evidence that the person signing the DS1 had authority to do so on behalf of the bank. Mr & Mrs Turner continued their fraud by supplying the defendant with a purported power of attorney apparently appointing four individuals, including one whose name and signature was on the DS1 as the bank's attorneys. The power of attorney was also a fraudulent document but the defendant sent a certified copy of the purported power to HMLR who acted on it and removed the charge from the register. Two years after removal of the charge, the bank discovered that it had been removed and applied to alter the register to reinstate it. It was reinstated but ranking behind that of another lender who had subsequently taken a mortgage over the property. DB Bank sought and obtained indemnity from HMLR.

The causes of action brought by HMLR against the firm were firstly in negligence. It was alleged that the defendant owed a common law duty of care to the bank to take reasonable skill and care to verify that the form DS1 had been properly completed on behalf of the bank, that the other firm of solicitors had been instructed on its behalf, that the power of attorney was genuine, that the bank wished to discharge the charge and that the property was no longer charged as security for the payment of sums due under the charge. HMLR asserted that this duty was breached causing loss to the bank.

Secondly, and in the alternative, HMLR claimed negligent misrepresentation in that making the application for Mr & Mrs Turner in the way and using the documents which it did, the defendant expressly or impliedly represented to HMLR that it had taken sufficient steps or knew of sufficient facts to satisfy itself that the form DS1 had been properly executed on behalf of the bank, the other firm of solicitors had been instructed on behalf of the bank, the power of attorney was valid, the bank wished to discharge the charge, and that the property was no longer charged as security for the payment of the sums due under the charge. It was also asserted that the defendant owed HMLR a duty to take reasonable care that the representations were true.

The negligence argument failed. The court was not prepared to accept that the defendants owed a duty of care to the bank. The bank suffered loss not because the defendant had supplied the information to HMLR but rather because HMLR had removed the charge. Whilst this might seem like a somewhat delicate argument, conveyancers should take heart that the court was not prepared to accept that a duty of care was owed in the circumstances.

However, the negligent misrepresentation claim succeeded. The defendant knew or ought to have known that HMLR would rely on the documents and information submitted to it. In making the application to HMLR the defendant firm had assumed a duty to HMLR to make statements with reasonable care.

Conveyancers should therefore be concerned because the court was prepared to recognise that a duty of care is owed to HMLR when an application to HMLR is made. It is worth noting that the judge expressed doubts and was only 'narrowly persuaded' on the 'peculiar facts of this case' that the defendant had assumed a duty to take care in the representations which it made to HMLR.

Why is this case relevant?

This case demonstrates that it is possible for conveyancers to assume a duty of care when making an application to HMLR. Submitting an application to HMLR for registration based on a document which has been signed using the conveyancer-certified electronic signature procedure outlined in PG82 requires a named conveyancer to personally give a specific certificate to HMLR to confirm that HMLR's requirements have been met. This certificate is surely one which HMLR would seek to rely on in the event of fraud or HMLR incurring loss. The *Caffrey* case reminds us that the courts were prepared to find in favour of HMLR even in the absence of a specific certification which conveyancers will be required to give with conveyancer-certified electronic signatures.

Practice points

Conveyancers should think carefully about the steps to take when submitting a DS1 to HMLR. As a result of *Caffrey*, HMLR tightened its procedures to reduce fraud risk where a paper DS1 is submitted for the removal of a charge. Conveyancers might notice such applications are taking longer to conclude.

HMLR has also updated PG31 (discharge of charges) regarding identification requirements. Note in particular:

- HMLR will not accept forms DS1 and DS3 if sent by fax

- HMLR will not accept any alteration to forms DS1 or DS3 which is not provided for in the LRR 2003. In particular, neither form should be altered if money remains outstanding under the charge as a personal debt of the borrower

- An application to register a discharge in form DS1 must be made in form AP1 or form DS2, and an application to register a release in form DS3 must be made in form AP1

- Evidence of identity form ID1 or form ID2 will be required for the lender unless the lender is a UK bank or building society who sends HMLR the application itself, or it is represented by a conveyancer or the person lodging the application can confirm their identity

- Evidence of identity for an attorney signing a form DS1 or form DS3 on behalf of the lender is not required.

- Form ID1 or form ID2 will also be required for the person lodging the application is not a conveyancer (see PG67: evidence of identity)

Neocleous v Rees [2019] EWHC 2462 (Ch)

This is a County Court case which may strike fear into the hearts of conveyancers and litigators. The claimant sought specific performance of an alleged contract of compromise which involved a disposition of an interest in land. The defendant accepted that the contract would otherwise be enforceable but argued that the alleged contract failed to comply with the formalities required by s2 of the 1989 Act and was thus unenforceable. By way of reminder, s 2(1) states that:

> *"(1) A contract for the sale or other disposition of an interest in land can only be made in writing and only by incorporating all of the terms which the parties have expressly agreed in one document or, where contracts are exchanged, in each.*
>
> ...
>
> *(3) The documents incorporating the terms or, where contracts are exchanged, one of the documents incorporating them (but not necessarily the same one) must be signed by or on behalf of each party to the contract.*
>
> ..."

In the case, the alleged contract was contained in a string of emails. The facts revolved around a litigation matter and email discussions between the parties' solicitors which set out proposed settlement terms under which the claimants would buy a piece of land for £200,000 in full and final settlement of the claim. The offer was rejected and a further offer was made by email on the claimant's behalf to settle for £175,000.

It is worth pointing out the wording and format of the relevant emails.

"Dear Daniel, *Further to our telephone conversation I am pleased to confirm that terms of settlement between our respective clients have been reached on the following basis:*

(1) *Your clients will pay to my client the sum of £175,000 (one hundred and seventy-five thousand pounds – "the Settlement Sum") for the transfer of my client's jetty/boat landing plot/mooring (which is contained within title number CU67453) ("the Land") to Mr & Mrs Neocleous and the release of my client's right to pass and re-pass over the land used as a road and coloured brown on the conveyance dated 1 June 1945 between Poole (1) and Wootton (2) ("the Release").*

(2) *Although a date by which the Transfer and Release must have been completed has not been discussed, it has been agreed that your clients will use their best endeavours to complete the Transfer and Release as soon as possible.*

(3) *On completion of the Transfer and Release the Settlement Sum becomes payable immediately.*

(4) *The above is in full and final settlement of the Tribunal proceedings and any and all further claims between the parties. Our clients will bear their own legal costs of these proceedings and in respect of the Transfer and Release.*

I would be grateful if you would acknowledge receipt of this email and confirm your agreement to the above in order that I can then advise the Tribunal.

Many thanks

David Tear

Solicitor and Director

For and on behalf of AWB Charlesworth Solicitors"

(There followed contact details for Mr Tear.)

> The reply was as follows:
>
> "*Thank you for your email and I confirm my agreement with its contents.*
>
> *Kind regards*
>
> *Daniel*
>
> *Daniel Wise – Associate*
>
> *Dispute Resolution for and on behalf of Slater Heelis LLP*"
>
> (Again, there followed contact details)

Following the above exchange of emails, Mr Tear requested that a scheduled hearing be vacated and he agreed to prepare a consent order. The claimants put their solicitors in funds to pay £175,000 for the plot of land and a consent order was drafted which was marked 'subject to contract'. Amendments were made to the order and were emailed back which was headed 'without prejudice and subject to contract'.

The defendants argued that the matter be re-listed for hearing, their position being that the terms of settlement had not been finalised between the parties. The claimants then issued proceedings seeking specific performance of what they alleged was a contract of compromise. The claimants alleged that the email exchange amounted to a binding contract of compromise. They argued that since the agreement involved the disposition of an interest in land, it must satisfy s 2 and contended that the two emails amounted to a single document which were signed by or on behalf of each party and thus the formalities of the 1989 Act were met.

The defendants argued that there was no enforceable contract under the 1989 Act because:

1. the emails did not show an intention to create an agreement for the disposition in land; rather they showed an intention to reduce their settlement into writing

2. the emails did not contain all of the terms of the alleged agreement since the parties had expressed an intention to reduce such terms to writing in a further document (namely the consent order) and

3. the emails were not signed by the parties

The defendants conceded the first and second points so at trial the only issue between the parties to be decided was whether the signature requirement of s 2(3) had been met.

The defendant asserted that the first email referred to above did not add the signatory's name at the bottom of the email, instead it was automatically added as an email footer. The defendant's solicitors used Microsoft Outlook for the management of emails and the policy of the solicitors was to have an 'automatic footer' applied to the end of every email sent from the firm such that, if an email was created, the following words would appear "*David Tear, Solicitor and Director, For and on behalf of AWB Charlesworth Solicitors*" followed by his contact details. The firm accepted that the use of the words 'many thanks' above the footer in the first email above was sufficient to give authority to the email.

The claimants contended that the typed name of the sender at the foot of an email, whether entered by the sender or generated by the software used to manage emails rendered the document as 'signed' within the meaning of s 2(1) so long as the inclusion of the name was for the purpose of giving authenticity to the documents. The claimants relied on a statement in J *Pereira Fernandes SA v Mehta* [2016] 1 WLR 1543 in which it was said:

> '*I have no doubt that if a party creates and sends an electronically created document then he will be treated as having signed it to the same extent that he would in law as having signed a hard copy of the same document. The fact that the document is created electronically as opposed to as a hard copy can make no difference... [31] ... if a party or a party's agent sending an email types his or her or his or her principals' name to the extent required or permitted by existing case law in the body of an email, then in my view that would be sufficient signature for the purposes of section 4 (of the Statute of Frauds 1677)." [HH Judge Pelling, para 31]*'

Helpfully, the judge also summarised various aspects which are of direct relevance to the development of electronic signatures in conveyancing as follows:

> *36. In any event, the Claimants draw attention to academic criticism of the judgment in Firstpost by the authors of Emmet and Farrand on Title, at paragraph 2.041.01, criticism which was noted by the Law Commission in Consultation Paper No. 237, "Electronic Execution of Documents" at paragraph 3.58.*
>
> *37. The Consultation Paper considers various authorities as well as the E-Signatures Directive 1999/93/EC, domestic legislation in the form of the Electronic Communication Act 2000 giving effect to the E-Signatures Directive and the Electronic Identification, Authentication and Trust Services (eIDAS) Regulation 910/2014. All three of these seek to give electronic signatures similar effect to a handwritten signature, but none purports to determine whether an electronic signature is capable of satisfying an existing statutory signature requirement and indeed Article 2(3) of eIDAS provides that the regulation "does not affect national or Union law related to the conclusion and validity of contract or other legal or procedural obligations relating to form."*
>
> *38. It is however relevant to note the definition of electronic signature within these instruments:*
>
> *i) Article 2(1) of the E-Signatures Directive defines "electronic signature" as "data in electronic form which are attached to or logically associated with other electronic data and which serve as a method of authentication";*
>
> *ii) Section 7 of the Electronic Communications Act 2000 as enacted defined "electronic signature" as*
>
> *"anything in electronic form as*
>
> *(a) is incorporated into or otherwise logically associated with electronic communication or electronic data; and*

(b) purports to be so incorporated or associated for the purpose of being used in establishing the authenticity of the communication or data, the integrity of the communication or data or both."[3]

iii) Article 3(10) of eIDAS define "electronic signature" as data in electronic form which is attached to or logically associated with other data in electronic form and which is used by the signatory to sign"

39. It should be noted that the emphasis in terms of definition of "electronic signature" is not on the form of the signature (for example, whether it is a facsimile of handwriting or whether as here it is typed form) but rather on its purpose, namely to authenticate or to sign.

40. The Law Commission Consultation Paper concludes at paragraph 3.80 that: "The review of the case law above demonstrates that electronic signatures have been found to satisfy a statutory requirement for a signature where there has been evidence of an intention to authenticate the document. Such findings have been made under the Law of Property Miscellaneous Provisions Act 1989, the Consumer Credit Act 1974 and the Statute of Frauds 1677. A finding of validity of an electronic signature does not appear to be limited to a particular type of signature – a typed name at the end of an email is sufficient, as is clicking an "I accept" button on a website. It has been suggested that an email header may not be sufficient. However, it is arguable that even this may function as a signature if there was sufficient evidence to demonstrate an intention to authenticate the document."

41. The Law Commission Report goes on to consider whether amendment is required to Section 2 of the 1989 Act to make provision for electronic signature and concludes that it is not necessary, stating:

"Our provisional view is that the combination of EU law, statute and case law means that, under the current law, an electronic

signature is capable of meeting a statutory requirement for a signature if an authenticating intention can be demonstrated."

42. The Claimants contend that the key to understanding Section 2 of the 1989 Act is to appreciate the policy behind the Act – the requirement for a single document (which as here can include a chain of emails) which contains signatures from both parties authenticating the agreement in the document. The focus then is on the appearance of an intention to authenticate. Where, as here, a party types an email which ends "Many Thanks" knowing that the computer upon which it is typed will automatically include the sender's name after the text, there is a clear indication of an intention to authenticate.'

The court pointed out that the issue to be decided was whether an automatically generated signature at the foot of an email applied the name with authenticating intent. The court considered that the manual typing rather than the automatic inclusion of the words 'many thanks' at the end of the email strongly suggested that the author was relying on the automatic footer to sign off his name. The court said that looked at objectively, the presence of the name indicates a clear intention to associate oneself with the email – to authenticate it or to sign it.

The court rejected the argument that a 'signature' had to be hand written (whether scanned or inserted electronically) and was therefore prepared to hold that the relevant email was signed on behalf of the defendant and as such, the claimant was entitled to the order for specific performance.

Why is this case relevant?

The case is part of a growing body of evidence that the courts are prepared to accept electronically generated signatures as being valid. This is even where the signature at the footer of an email is generated automatically. Of course, this is only a County Court decision meaning that it is not binding on another County Court or the High Court. However, it nonetheless should be of concern to conveyancers because, for many years, conveyancers have probably been of the view that an exchange of letters or, more recently, emails, was not capable of creating a contract for the sale of land.

The case is of broader relevance to conveyancers than merely acceptance by HMLR of conveyancer-certified electronic signatures but it is a crucial reminder to conveyancers that, in certain circumstances, the contract for the sale of land can be created by email. It is probably fair to say that the majority of conveyancers transact by email, many of which will have automatically generated signature footers.

Practice points

To mitigate against the risk of an exchange of emails creating a contract for the sale of an interest in land, conveyancers may wish to consider the following:

- whether a review of the use of automatically generated signatures in email footers is desirable

- whether all communications, including emails, should resurrect the use of the words 'subject to contract' (which many practitioners had stopped using as a matter of course following the introduction of the 1989 Act)

- whether the words 'subject to contract' should be added to all emails automatically

- whether, to be belt and braces, wording to the following effect should be added beneath every automatically generated signature in an email footer: 'Please note that nothing in this communication is intended to bind our client and all matters remain strictly subject to contract'

It is fair to say that the use of the term 'subject to contract' is not completely watertight in that an agreement which otherwise satisfies s 2 of the 1989 Act may be enforceable even if the term is used. However, as a general safety net it must make sense for conveyancers to reintroduce this wording at least until a higher court considers the matter. It is worth mentioning of course that the case was brought in the context of a litigation matter. Thus, these issues and concerns are of equal relevance to practitioners working in that department.

Athena Brands Ltd v Superdrug Stores Plc [2019] EWHC 3503 (Comm)

In the light of *Neocleous,* the above case is worthy of mention. It is a commercial rather than land law case but in brief, the High Court concluded that an exchange of emails between two of the most well-known brands on the high street was capable of giving rise to a contract for the purchase of goods worth over £1.3 million. As with the *Neocleous* case, an email chain between persons in each of the organisations took place to discuss arrangements for supply of a particular product range.

An email was sent which included the words 'please go ahead with the below'. It was not in dispute that this referred to the preceding email chain. The products sold much more slowly than had been anticipated and, on that basis, Superdrug emailed to indicate that 'orders going forward would be unlikely' and indeed they did not place any further orders. Athena sought to recover its losses from the shortfall in the minimum quantities which it alleged Superdrug had agreed to purchase which put the claim at just under £980,000 plus storage charges for unsold stock and interest.

The judge summarised a central point of the case rather succinctly:

> *'Starting with the question of construction, the relevant law is also not in dispute. The court engages in an objective exercise to determine the meaning of the words in which an agreement, or alleged agreement, has been expressed, to determine what a reasonable independent person would consider them to have intended. In doing so it may have regard to that surrounding circumstances or factual matrix in which the words have been used, to determine whether the parties intended some meaning other than the ordinary meaning of those words. Any question whether the parties intended to enter into legal relations is to be similarly objectively determined. An employee has ostensible authority to enter into transactions binding on his employer to the extent held out by the employer, either expressly or by implication from what would normally be expected of an employee in a similar position. A party relying on such ostensible authority must also show that they reasonably relied on that authority in entering into the transaction in question.'* [HHJ David Cooke, para 29]

What is very interesting about the judgement is that there is very little discussion as to whether the exchange of emails per se was capable of creating a binding contract, as there seemed to be a tacit acceptance that the email exchange could, of itself, create a contract. A significant portion of the judgement was taken up with considering the standard purchase terms of Superdrug and whether or not the employee involved had the authority to order stock.

Why is this case relevant?

This case is further evidence of the willingness of the courts to accept electronic communications as a means of creating valid contracts. As indicated above, this case does not relate to the sale and purchase of land but the general principle is still of interest to conveyancers.

Practice points

Any organisation, not just a law firm, should review its procedures relating to the discussion/negotiation by employees relating to the purchase of any goods. It is fair to say that with many more staff working at home, the use of email to discuss such acquisitions is likely to produce a continuing risk. The following issues should be considered:

- who in an organisation has authority to commit the organisation to entering into contracts? This authority must be made clear to any potential contractor
- including wording such as 'subject to contract' or making it clear on the face of an email that the sender does not have authority to bind the organisation into a contract is important
- training for all employees in this area is vital

Wood v Commercial First Business Ltd (In Liquidation) [2019] EWHC 2205 (Ch)

This case considered the rather specific issue of the status of commission paid to a mortgage broker. This is not the specific point which is relevant to conveyancers in the context of considering conveyancer-certified electronic signatures. What is of interest here is the fact that the court considered the circumstances surrounding the execution of a deed and specifically the witnessing requirements.

The facts of the case centred around a borrower who was seeking to challenge the validity (and thus enforceability) of two commercial mortgages. Clearly it would be to the borrower's advantage to have a court declare that one or both of them was not valid and thus not binding. One argument put forward by the borrower was that one of the mortgage deeds had not been properly executed because the attesting witness had not signed the mortgage deed at the same time as the borrower.

By way of reminder, s 1(3) of the 1989 Act states:

> *(3) An instrument is validly executed as a deed by an individual if, and only if—*
>
> > *(a) it is signed—*
> >
> > > *(i) by him in the presence of a witness who attests the signature; or*
> > >
> > > *(ii) at his direction and in his presence and the presence of two witnesses who each attest the signature; and*
> >
> > *(b) it is delivered as a deed*

The instrument will thus only be validly executed as a deed if the deed is signed in the presence of a witness who attests the signature. The circumstances in the case are that the borrower did not dispute the fact that the witness was in her presence when she had signed the deed, but the witness had added their signature etc to the mortgage deed at a later point in time. In addition, the witness had added their signature and details without the borrower being present. The borrower argued that the 1989 Act required the signatory and the witness to both be in each other's presence and that they should both sign in each other's presence.

The court disagreed with this view and held that the mortgage deed had been validly executed despite the fact that the witness had signed and added their details later on. The court observed that the 1989 Act only required the witness to be in the presence of the signatory and if it had been the intention to require the witness and signatory to sign at the same time and in each other's presence, then the 1989 Act would have included this provision but it did not.

Why is this case relevant?

In confirming that it will accept conveyancer-certified electronic signatures on deeds submitted for registration, HMLR has brought signing and witnessing procedures into sharp focus. The case is a reminder that the failure by the witness to sign their name and details on the deed at the same time as witnessing the signatory sign their own name, will not necessarily invalidate the deed from the perspective of the 1989 Act. However, conveyancers should remember that the longer the period of time between the signatures, the greater the possibility for an argument about the validity of the deed.

Practice points

We have seen that HMLR has suggested that in the context of conveyancer-certified electronic signatures, both conveyancers should retain with their conveyancing file a copy of the electronic audit report produced by the platform used by the seller's conveyancer at the end of the signing process. This should capture the time that the signatory and witness added their details to the deed.

The buyer's conveyancer should consider obtaining an undertaking from the seller's conveyancer to produce this audit report prior to completion to give the buyers conveyancer the opportunity to check the timings of the addition of the electronic signatures to the deed. If there appears to be a significant period of time between the signatory adding their signature and the witness adding their signature, the buyer's conveyancer may consider raising a query about the signing and witnessing process prior to releasing the completion funds. Remember that either conveyancer is required to certify in their own name that, to the best of their knowledge, HMLR's requirements as set out in section 3.2 of PG82 have been met.

Yuen v Wong [2020] First Tier Tribunal (Property Chamber) ref 2016/1089

As we have seen, s 1(3) of the 1989 Act requires a deed to be witnessed and attested. In the above case, the FTT had to consider whether remote witnessing of a signature via Skype was sufficient to meet this requirement.

The case involved the transfer of a property and an allegation that a signature had been forged or alternatively, if it had not been forged then it had not been validly witnessed. A transfer had been signed by parties in Hong Kong, one signature had been witnessed by a solicitor who joined the meeting via Skype from London and witnessed the signature remotely. The FTT considered that it was arguable that the witnessing was not valid because the witness was not in the physical presence of the signatory at the time of signing; they were only observing the signing via Skype. As it happens, the FTT did not have to decide on the point and is thus not binding authority.

Why is this case relevant?

The case reinforces the point which HMLR has taken in relation to conveyancer-certified electronic signatures that, for the time being at least, the signatory and the witness must be in each other's physical presence at the time the deed is signed.

What is interesting about the case is that the solicitor appears to have joined a meeting by Skype and not considered that their physical presence was required to validly witness the deed.

Conveyancers will no doubt be aware that their colleagues in the wills and probate department are for the time being at least, permitted to witness wills remotely due to the impact of the Covid-19 pandemic, but this relaxation of the witnessing requirements does not extend to the witnessing of a deed for the transfer of an interest in land.

Bioconstruct GmbH v Winspear and another [2020] EWHC 7 (QB)

In this case, the High Court had to consider the validity of the signing of a legal charge (which must be created by deed). The case involved the recovery of sums due under the terms of a deed of indemnity and security. A version of the deed in question had been signed by one party in the presence of a witness. Negotiations regarding the content of the deed continued after this signing resulting in a final version being produced which incorporated a number of significant changes to the earlier version which had been signed. At the completion meeting, the signature page from the earlier version of the deed was simply transferred to the final version. The court considered various other points of detail regarding signing and initialling amendments to the deed.

The court held that using pre-signed signature pages from an earlier draft of a deed meant that there was no valid execution of the deed.

Why is this case relevant?

It is an important reminder for conveyancers not to 'recycle' earlier signature pages and add them to subsequent versions of the relevant document. Doing so could invalidate the entire document.

Practice points

Conveyancers will note that in the Mercury signing instructions, it is necessary for the final version of the document to be sent to the signatory for them to print off the signature page. For the Mercury signing process to work, the signatory must then attach their scanned, signed signature page to an email along with the original deed and send it back to their conveyancer.

Similarly, step 1 of the conveyancer-certified electronic signatures process in PG82 specifically requires the conveyancer controlling the signing process to upload the final agreed copy of the deed (plus any plans) to the platform.

Whilst this issue is less likely to arise where the transfer document is a straightforward transfer of the whole of the land in a registered title, a more complex transfer of part, or deed of easement, for example where the terms are still being negotiated between the parties could give rise to this issue. Conveyancers must never be tempted to substitute a pre-signed signature page on a version of a deed which is different to that which has been signed.

It highlights the importance again of the conveyancers thinking ahead to ensure that appropriate arrangements are in place for a final version of the completed document to be signed where some (or all) of the signatories are not physically present. Generally, these arrangements should not be hastily made on the day of completion itself even if the deed is to be signed using a conveyancer-certified electronic signature platform.

Summary of key issues for conveyancers arising from the above cases

1. Conveyancers can owe a duty of care to HMLR when making an application for registration; this should be kept in mind when considering the risk to the buyer's conveyancer of giving the certificate confirming compliance with PG82 (*Caffrey*)

2. More generally, conveyancers should consider what steps to take when submitting a DS1 to HMLR and should consider the terms of PG31 (*Caffrey*)

3. It is possible for the exchange of emails containing an automatically generated signature in the email footer to create a valid contract for the sale of an interest in land (*Neocleous)*

4. Firms should review the use of automatically generated signatures in email footers and consider whether to add the words 'subject to contract' and/or 'please note that nothing in this communication is intended to bind our client and all matters remains strictly subject to contract' in every automatically generated email footer (*Neocleous)*

5. An exchange of emails can create a contract for the sale and purchase of goods, irrespective of the authority of the parties to the emails (*Athena*)

6. Whilst a signatory and a witness have to be present at the same time, and the witness must see the signatory signing their name, the courts have recognised that the fact that the witness signed their own name and details at a later point in time (and not in the presence of the signatory) did not invalidate the deed. However best practice demands that the witness and the signatory both sign at the same time and in each other's presence (*Wood*)

7. If adopting the conveyancer-certified electronic signatures procedure, the buyer's conveyancer should consider requesting the electronic audit report produced by the platform used by the seller's conveyancer to review the time and date that the signatory and witness added their details to the deed. The buyer's conveyancer may consider seeking an undertaking from the seller's conveyancer to provide this prior to completion (*Wood*)

8. When signing a deed, the signatory and witness must be in each other's physical presence at the time the deed is signed and witnessing via remote electronic means (such as Skype or zoom) is not sufficient (*Yuen*)

9. Using pre-signed signature pages from an earlier draft of a deed may result in the deed being invalid (*Bioconstruct GmbH*)

CHAPTER SIX

RISK MANAGEMENT

Conveyancing firms are required to conduct regular and appropriate analysis of risk for regulatory and/or accreditation purposes. This analysis can either be on a firm wide basis, department wide basis or on individual files. This chapter is not intended to be a complete analysis of these areas because each firm will be subject to different requirements. However, it is important for firms to recognise that contracting with a platform provider and adopting conveyancer-certified electronic signatures should prompt the appropriate risk management review.

Let's consider some of the risks of wet ink and electronic signatures. Firms will have their own views as to the level of risks posed by each. There is further consideration of these issues in the Electronic Execution of Documents: Industry Working Group Interim Report

	Wet ink signatures	**Electronic signatures**
How do we know that the actual party has signed?	Reduced if conveyancer meets their client face to face and witnesses document signing Continuing risk if document is sent to client for signing Conveyancer should always check signature on documents received against the identification documents held on file	Reduced if platform provider also provides robust identification and AML procedures; particularly if biometrics are used Conveyancers may face a risk if identification and AML is carried out via a different provider/system than the conveyancer-certified electronic signature procedure Risk reduced due to two factor authentication

How do we know that an actual witness has signed?	Eliminated if conveyancer witnesses the signature Continuing risk if document is sent to client for signing	Risk reduced due to two factor authentication to be sent via the platform to a different device Risks regarding identity of witnesses is likely to be reduced generally using electronic signatures because the conveyancer needs to know who they are in advance and have their mobile number to enable HMLR's PG82 requirements to be met
How do we know that the witness and signatory were present at the same time?	Eliminated if conveyancer witnesses the signature Continuing risk if document is sent to client for signing	Mitigated by conveyancer ensuring that specific instructions are sent to the signatory prior to signing process Conveyancer will need to have witness contact details prior to signing process, instructions can be given to the witness Wording can be added to the transfer to confirm that the witness and signatory were present at the same time Buyer's conveyancers should check the audit report for the time and date that the signatory and witness signed using the electronic platform

General fraud risk	Reduced if conveyancer meets their client face to face and witnesses document signing	Conveyancer must be satisfied regarding compromise or hacking risk when sourcing a platform provider <u>Other fraud concerns</u>: It is possible for a fraudster to set up a number of email addresses Obtaining a new mobile phone and SIM is easy Email interception remains a real risk for firms Identity theft
General signing risk	Continuing risk if document is sent to client for signing	Simply copying, pasting or typing a signature into an electronic document has a significant fraud or error risk – mitigated as HMLR has specific requirements for conveyancer-certified electronic signatures
Risk that signatory does not know what they were signing, rendering the deed invalid	Considerably reduced if the conveyancer meets the client face-to-face, explains the risk and keeps a contemporaneous attendance note	Remains a risk because it is unlikely that the signatory will receive a detailed explanation of the content of the document at the time of signing

	Reduced if the conveyancer sends a letter/report of explanation with the documents to be signed and returned	Mitigated by ensuring that a letter/report is sent well before the signing process which the client should be asked to acknowledge in writing and confirm they have understood Further mitigated if a 'read and understood' receipt is generated by the platform at the time of signature. Consider also requiring client to 'sign' their name using a stylus or pen
General risk of fraudulent document being produced for registration	This is an ever-present risk. In the light of *Caffrey,* conveyancers should not take documents presented to them at face value and should take steps to be satisfied as to origin, authenticity and signatures. If in doubt, such a document should not be presented to HMLR for registration	It is possible that a document could be provided to a conveyancer that looks as if it has been produced on a platform but has not. Acceptance of such a document and presentation for registration would mean that the buyer's conveyancer had done virtually no due diligence and would be recklessly giving the certification to HMLR required by PG82. To mitigate this risk further, the buyer's conveyancer should always insist on receiving the platform generated audit report along with the deed

How to approach the risk review

If a conveyancing firm has a dedicated risk manager or risk department, then the contents of this section might not be relevant to that firm. This section is aimed at busy conveyancers who do not have dedicated risk management support within the organisation and who may need some guidance on some of the issues to take into account when considering whether to adopt conveyancer-certified electronic signatures and, if so, which platform provider to use.

All conveyancing firms should have a compliance plan and risk report. This is where they should start. Contracting with a new platform provider and introducing a new procedure for conveyancing transactions is likely to impact on the following areas of a compliance plan:

- undertakings
- new staff/contractors
- regulatory deadlines
- risk management
- conduct issues
- supervision
- staff training and development
- outsourcing

A good starting point for a firm considering platform providers and conveyancer-certified electronic signatures would be to consider the following:

1. Your work – what type of conveyancing work do you do and what are the particular risks? How do you mitigate those risks? Do you need to meet regulatory and other requirements (eg. CQS?)

2. Your infrastructure – define your reporting lines and consider how risks are identified, managed and mitigated.

3. Your people – who has responsibility for risk in the conveyancing department? Is this the same person as the COLP/COFA?

4. Your policies – are they effective and appropriate to your type and size of firm? How are policies communicated, applied and updated?

5. Your controls – what controls are in place to mitigate the risk in your conveyancing team, are they appropriate for the size of the firm and how does your firm assess and monitor the effectiveness of those controls?

6. Your training – how does your firm identify and meet the training needs of your conveyancing team?

Conduct, regulations and accreditations

A conveyancing firm will need to consider the impact of introducing conveyancer-certified electronic signatures and the consequent risk assessment and training needs on conduct and regulatory requirements in addition to any accreditations. Some examples are shown in the table below, but there may be others.

CLC REGULATED FIRMS	
Code of conduct *Overriding principle* *2. Maintain high standards of work*	Introducing a significant new procedure will impact on this principle which conveyancers must ensure they maintain
CLC regulated firms are obliged to: • *systematically identify and mitigate risks to the business and to clients*	These outcomes point to the importance of ensuring that any risks of introducing a platform provider and conveyancer-certified electronic signatures are appropriately identified, managed

• *maintain proper governance, management, supervision, financial and risk management arrangements and controls* • *systematically identify, monitor and manage risks to the delivery of the code's outcomes* • *maintain proper records to evidence their arrangements and how they are applied*	and monitored. Conveyancers should also ensure that discussions and decisions are properly recorded and the evidence retained.
CLC firms must comply with the anti-money laundering and combating terrorist financing code which requires the firm to: • *systematically identify and mitigate risks to the business and to clients* • *ensure that the management arrangements, systems and controls enable the identification, assessment, monitoring and management of AML/CTF risk and are appropriate to the nature, scale and complexity of their activities. Any system or product the firm uses must be sufficiently robust to provide the necessary degree of certainty and incorporate qualitative checks that assess the strength of information supplied. It will include data from a range of sources and across time. The firm's evidence-base must be composite and comprehensive. The firm must carry out regular reviews of the adequacy of management arrangements, systems and controls*	This is the broad AML requirement but conveyancers are reminded that a new platform provider may provide AML services or link into the firm's existing case management system and it must thus be 'sufficiently robust'. Conveyancers will need to consider the impact of a new platform on existing systems.

CLC firms are required to ensure that their records are stored on 'durable medium' – *'the method by which information is stored in a way accessible for future reference (for no less than the period prescribed by the CLC) and which allows the unchanged reproduction of the information stored'*	Central to HMLR's requirements for conveyancer-certified electronic signatures is the electronic audit report which must also meet these regulatory standards.
© CLC	
SRA REGULATED FIRMS	
3 Service and competence *3.6 You ensure that the individuals you manage are competent to carry out their role, and keep their professional knowledge and skills, as well as understanding of their legal, ethical and regulatory obligations, up to date.*	This is a reminder of the need to ensure that all people in a conveyancing team are adequately trained to use a new system
6.3 *You keep the affairs of current and former clients confidential unless disclosure is required or permitted by law or the client consents*	Conveyancers must ensure that clients give their consent for any information held about them in the audit trail on the platform to be passed to the conveyancer acting for the other party, where appropriate
© SRA	

<table>
<tr><th colspan="2">LEXCEL ACCREDITED FIRMS</th></tr>
<tr><td>The current version is Lexcel v6.1 although the Law Society indicates on its website that existing publications have not yet been updated to reflect v6.1. The following elements of the case management checklist are of particular relevance:<ul><li>documents must be identifiable and traceable and be stored in an orderly way</li><li>practices must have an information management and security policy which includes information on how practices ensure that information is kept confidential</li><li>practices must have an email policy</li><li>practices must have policies and procedures governing the risks in delivering advice, including supervision and outsourcing</li><li>the firm's risk register and compliance plan will need review</li><li>there is a specific requirement for practices to have a policy in relation to outsourced activities</li></ul></td><td>Introducing a new platform provider and conveyancer-certified electronic signature process will impact on all of the listed areas</td></tr>
</table>

CONVEYANCING QUALITY SCHEME (CQS) CQS is a Law Society quality standard for residential conveyancing practices. A CQS accredited firm must be authorised and regulated by the SRA. A significant part of the accreditation is for the conveyancing firm to demonstrate that they have standardised processes in place to recognise and reduce risks. Accredited firms have to ensure that all relevant persons complete mandatory training. Firms which have the accreditation must adopt the protocol and follow the Core Practice Management Standards (CPMS). These were updated in February 2022 and CQS accredited firms had to ensure compliance from 1 May 2022. If a firm already has the Lexcel accreditation, they will already have met some of the required CPMS. Of particular relevance to CQS accredited firms which are considering sourcing a conveyancer-certified electronic signatures platform provider are the following standards:	
Section 1 requires firms to have documentation setting out the management structure which designates the responsibilities of individuals and their accountability. This includes the obligation to have a business continuity plan. A risk management policy which includes a risk register and compliance plan. Firms must define risk management responsibilities and effectively communicate risk information	All of these areas will require review

Section 3 relates to information management. This includes the requirement to have an information management and security policy	This will be central to entering into any contract with a platform provider. The guidance sets out some key issues including how practices ensure that information is kept confidential, its integrity is maintained and that it is accessible. The policy must encompass information that is held electronically and physically. The guidance suggests that a register might set out the type of information and whether it is paper or digital, and where/how those assets are kept securely and for how long. This aspect of the CQS relates to the confidentiality and GDPR aspects of the audit report both in terms of obtaining the client's consent to release their details to the other conveyancer in addition to obtaining the information and consent of witnesses who, generally, will not be clients of the firm. Interestingly, the guidance states as follows: *'While there is no requirement currently that plans, policies and procedures, registers and records will be in electronic format, practices are encouraged to do so. This is because records and registers are easier to curate, supervise and share when held digitally.'*

Section 4 deals with people management	The guidance states that conveyancers should be kept up to date with the latest guidance, articles and case law relating to residential conveyancing, client care and risk management. Clearly any training on the introduction of conveyancer-certified electronic signatures would be essential
Section 5 deals with risk management and specifies that practices must have a risk management policy which includes: • a compliance plan • a risk register • defined risk management roles and responsibilities • arrangements for communicating risk information	The guidance points out that the risk register typically identifies current and emerging risks facing the practice and explains how they are managed. The introduction of a new system would clearly require a detailed review of the risk register and involvement of the risk manager and training to ensure that all members of a conveyancing team understand the new risks and reporting arrangements. Interestingly, even firms that do not decide to adopt conveyancer-certified electronic signatures may need to review their procedures to ensure that they comply with the requirement to decline work if it falls outside acceptable risk levels. For example, if the seller's conveyancer insists on providing a transfer signed using a platform provider and the buyer's conveyancer does not agree, the latter may have to consider declining to act in that particular transaction.

	Whether adopting the new process will not, all CQS firms should consider adding conveyancer-certified electronic signatures to their generic list of conveyancing risks. All relevant staff in the conveyancing team should be appropriately trained
Section 7 deals with file and case management and includes the requirement that firms can identify and trace any documents, files, deeds, wills or any other items relating to a matter. It also includes the requirement to have a procedure to safeguard the confidentiality of matter files and all other client information	This aspect of the CQS is relevant to the production of the audit report and the risks relating to confidentiality, GDPR and the need to access and store the audit report. Adequate monitoring of documents which may only exist electronically is essential if a platform enabling conveyancer-certified electronic signatures is to be introduced We have seen that the production of the platform audit report and conveyancer's certificate could mean that client (and/or witness) details are sent to the conveyancer on the other side of the transaction. Obtaining the client's consent to maintain confidentiality obligations is essential The guidance makes it clear that all records, documents and correspondence should generally be capable of being traced and this requirement applies equally to hard copy and electronic files.

	Please see Chapter 4 for consideration of issues relating to electronic storage of documents by a third-party platform provider

Additional Support

Firms that do not have dedicated risk managers or departments are likely to need additional guidance or support. The National Cyber Security Centre (NCSC) has a lot of guidance available for firms. Of particular relevance in the current context is:

Cloud security guidance

The NCSC suggests that the following steps should be worked through to assist an organisation to identify cloud services which are suitably secure for their intended use.

1 Know your business requirements

Understand your intended use of the cloud service. Consider issues such as availability and connectivity. Identify those risks which would be unacceptable to your organisation should they be realised, and those that would not.

2 Understand your information

Identify the information that will be processed, stored or transported by the cloud service. Understand the legal and regulatory implications. For example, if personal data is to be stored or processed, then the Data Protection Act should be considered.

3 Determine relevant security principles

You now know your business requirements, you've identified the risks you are/aren't willing to take. And you have a clear picture of the information which will be exposed to the service.

With this information you should be able to determine which of the Cloud Security principles are most relevant to your planned use of the service.

4 Understand how the principles are implemented

Find out how the cloud service claims to implement the security principles you've identified as relevant. Different approaches will result in different risks for you to consider. Our detailed guide to implementing the cloud security principles will help you with this.

5 Understand the level of assurance offered

Can the service provider demonstrate that the principles you identified in ***step 3*** *have been implemented correctly?*

Some suppliers offer little more than promises, others provide contracts, and some engage certified, independent assessors to validate their claims.

6 Identify additional mitigations you can apply

Consider any additional measures your organisation (as a consumer of the cloud service) can apply to help reduce risk to your applications and information.

7 Consider residual risks

Having worked through the above steps, decide whether any remaining risks are acceptable.

8 Continue to monitor and manage the risks

Once in use, periodically review whether the service still meets your business and security needs.

The NCSC has published excellent risk management guidance to help organisations make decisions about cybersecurity risk. Even those firms which have IT support (whether in-house or an external provider) should take responsibility for considering risk management in a conveyancing context.

> *Accept some risk*
>
> *When you've made a business decision (such as deploying some new technology in your organisation) you will have to accept some possibility that it could be attacked, subverted, destroyed or otherwise messed with. We all experience risk because the future is uncertain, and cyber risk is no different.*
>
> *We're **not** saying that you should just shrug your shoulders and ignore cyber risks, rather you need to focus on those risks which you can practically do something about. Getting this right depends on:*
>
> - *understanding what you expect to gain by taking a given risk*
> - *how much it would hurt you if that risk was realised*
> - *how much you can afford to spend on protecting yourself*
>
> *This all comes down to judgement. So if anyone tells you that a particular framework or piece of security technology can manage 'all of your cyber risks', take everything they say with a pinch of salt. You'd be amazed how often the NCSC hear this claim.*
>
>

Other issues for firms to consider

Risks regarding the use of email

In cybercrime terms, the use of email represents one of the biggest risks to firms. The interception of email traffic between law firms and their clients is well known. The possibility that client bank account details or the firm's own account details can be intercepted and swapped for those of a fraudster is well documented. This risk is the reason that most firms will telephone the recipients of telegraphic transfer payments to verify bank account details.

Conveyancing firms may wish to consider whether they should move to the use of encrypted emails to mitigate this basic and very prevalent cybercrime.

Indemnity Insurers

Firms may consider liaising with their professional indemnity insurer as appropriate as part of their risk analysis when considering adopting conveyancer-certified electronic signatures. The insurers may have specific requirements regarding IT, security and cybercrime risks. It may be that the insurers consider the adoption of a conveyancer-certified electronic signatures platform to be a positive thing in terms of risk management which may impact on the firm's indemnity insurance premium.

Cybercrime and the platform provider

This Practical Guide is not specifically about the risks of cybercrime – those risks are sufficient to justify a book in their own right. However, firms should consider cybercrime risks more generally when considering adopting the conveyancer-certified electronic signature procedure.

- Security of the system generally – when reviewing the electronic signature platforms that are available, conveyancing firms should ensure that they understand the security procedures that the platform providers have in place.

- What are the risks of the system being hacked?

- What are the risks of seller fraud?

- If the platform provider proposes using a cloud-based storage system, the conveyancing firm should be confident that it is secure and should look at the accreditation of potential cloud suppliers. The SRA suggests that firms should understand what they are responsible for, such as making sure the privacy settings are appropriate

Certification of documents

Where electronic documents are used, in general terms, conveyancers should be wary of the risk of certifying documents for registration. It can now be very difficult to distinguish a copy from an original document. Conveyancers should take care to ensure that they know the origin of a document which they are submitting for registration. When lodging applications for registration via the HMLR portal, firms must choose the correct certification statement for each document uploaded or the application may be delayed. The three options for certification are:

1. I/We certify this attachment is a true copy of the original

2. I/We certify this attachment is a true copy of a document which is certified by a conveyancer to be a true copy of the original

3. This attachment is an uncertified copy

Liability in the event of fraud

A concern for conveyancers will be to establish where liability lies in the event that a platform enabling conveyancer-certified electronic signatures is hacked or subject to fraud. HMLR's concern would be that a fraud gives rise to a mistake in the register. A fraud might prevent registration or if the registration had taken place, a void transfer would result in a mistaken register. This is clearly an area which would be fact dependent and could be complex. If a fraudster was impersonating someone else for example, this may have nothing to do with the platform service provider and the conveyancer-certified electronic signature itself. So, a detailed analysis of the nature and root of any fraud would need to be carried out to establish the source and where the liability should lie.

Despite the fact that HMLR has mandated the use of conveyancer-certified electronic signatures, HMLR is not endorsing a particular platform provider and thus if HMLR suffered loss (as in *Caffrey* – see Chapter 5), then they may well seek to recover any losses from the conveyancer submitting the application for registration (see PG39).

HMLR has indicated publicly that it is not making any change to its practice or recourse as a result of introducing electronic signatures. They have said that *'legal responsibility between the law firm and the signature provider we presume will be considered in the supply contract'.*

Conveyancers are again reminded of the *Dreamvar* case. The warranty of authority point was discussed in Chapter 2. But there is another very relevant aspect of the case which concerns the interrelationship between conveyancer's liability and their indemnity insurance.

In considering the case, the Court of Appeal found that the buyer's solicitors, Mishcon de Reya, had taken all reasonable steps in the conveyancing transaction and were not negligent. However, Mishcon de Reya held the completion money on trust for their buyer client and when it was paid away for a completion which was in fact based on fraud, the firm were held to be in breach of trust. When considering whether Mishcon de Reya should be granted relief against the breach of trust claim (under s 61 Trustee Act 1925) the Court of Appeal endorsed the view of the trial judge who said:

> *'"187. As for MdR's position, it is common ground that it is insured for events such as this, and that its insurance cover is sufficient to cover in full the loss suffered, should it not be excused from liability. In terms of balancing the relative effects or consequences of the breach of trust, it is apparent that MdR (with or without insurance) is far better able to meet or absorb it than Dreamvar.'*

The Court of Appeal found this view 'unimpeachable' [para 110].

What the Court of Appeal effectively said therefore is that because they were properly insured, Mishcon de Reya should meet the cost of the fraud (albeit their right to pursue the seller's conveyancer was reinstated by the Court of Appeal). Conveyancers should keep this aspect of the *Dreamvar* judgement in mind when considering the safeguards which a platform provider might reasonably be expected to have in place to guard against the possibility of fraud and hacking.

Throughout this Practical Guide we would remind conveyancers that risk cannot be eliminated. The best that conveyancers can hope to achieve is to mitigate the risk. Many conveyancers would take the view that a two-factor authentication, cloud-based signature process actually offers greater safety than the traditional wet signature approach. This is an assessment for each conveyancing firm to make and will depend on such factors as:

- the firm's client base
- whether the firm meets the majority of its clients face-to-face (in a non-pandemic situation)
- whether its clients are likely to have the appropriate technology to readily embrace conveyancer-certified electronic signatures. Remember that vulnerable or older clients might not have access to email or a suitable mobile phone
- the firm's existing case management system or conveyancing processes
- the firm's own attitude to the use of technology in conveyancing
- the firm's own IT procedures, support, firewalls and general level of sophistication
- the firm's attitude to risk

Where does this leave conveyancers?

As ever, it leaves conveyancers being the only fully insured party and thus exposed to the risk of meeting the cost of fraud or loss, whether incurred by their client, the other party or HMLR.

There is inherent risk in changing from one procedure to another and human error can never be eliminated, however sophisticated a system.

Remember that the LSAG makes a universal point in relation to electronic verification of clients:

> *'As technology has developed, use of electronic identification and verification (EID&V) tools have become more common. While you can never outsource your ultimate responsibility, EID&V tools can be useful in protecting your practice. '(para 6.14.3)*
>
> *'EID&V is also sensitive to human error, and mistakes of data input can lead to the incorrect individual being checked. Practices should consider the risks of this and how they mitigate, e.g., dip sampling past files to check accuracy, ideally by another individual at the practice. Practices should also be alert to any surprising results that may indicate human error at the data input stage.' (Para 7.3)*

These points are just as relevant to choosing a platform provider and implementing a system of electronic signatures of documents.

Any platform must produce evidence of the timing and dating of a document which must be signed, witnessed, delivered, dated in the correct order and all relevant stages accurately timed.

When sourcing a conveyancer-certified electronic signature platform provider, conveyancers may wish to establish whether the provider has any form of indemnity insurance in place to protect the conveyancer in the event of the system being hacked or compromised. Presumably if the provider is very confident that their system is secure, they may feel able to offer conveyancing firms some form of insurance. This may be a factor which persuades a conveyancing firm to use one provider over another.

CHAPTER SEVEN

THE FUTURE

In this chapter we will briefly consider the ongoing work in relation to electronic signatures and will attempt to draw a conclusion for conveyancers in relation to the identification of a platform provider and adoption of conveyancer-certified electronic signatures.

As a general observation, the drive towards further digitisation of the land registration process, of which electronic signatures is a part, is the announcement by HMLR that as from November 2022 digital applications for straightforward applications will be mandatory. The Digital Registration Service (DRS) was launched in April 2021 to enable customers who use the HMLR portal to create and submit applications digitally. Electronic uploads will be switched off on 30 November 2022.

In parallel with developing and consulting on the conveyancer-certified electronic signatures project, HMLR is also working on Qualified Electronic Signatures which are a more advanced form of electronic signatures. HMLR has been working on a pilot for the development of Qualified Electronic Signatures and reported in Its blog (29.03.2022) that in September 2021, they registered their first deed using this process.

Qualified Electronic Signatures are a concept introduced by the eIDAS Directive. The identity of the signatory is identified through biometrics and this is how an electronic signature can be generated. The identification checks with conveyancer-certified electronic signatures are nowhere near as sophisticated as they will be if and when Qualified Electronic Signatures are introduced. The level of security is such that a witness is not required for a qualified electronic signature and the platform is provided by a trust provider.

HMLR is going to consult on the use of Qualified Electronic Signatures as a non-compulsory alternative to what is available at the moment, but it is fair to say that this will be a longer-term project and will probably involve other parts of government. Ultimately, if the identification and security processes with Qualified Electronic Signatures are such that liability for fraud or loss in the event that the system is compromised does not lie with conveyancers and their indemnity insurers, this may be a system which conveyancers would readily embrace.

s 91 LRA 2002 is potentially very significant because it allows for the creation and disposal of a legal estate by a document that is not a deed and thus it does not require witnessing. This would be a big step forward because it would replace deeds, not replicate them. This process would require identification verification and sophisticated encryption by a regulated Trust Service Provider and, at the moment, is in its infancy in England and Wales.

HMLR's Digital Identity Standard

HMLR has recognised the inconvenience and inconsistency of manually verifying the client's identity – for both conveyancers and their clients. HMLR, the Law Society, Cilex and CLC have recognised the potential for digital identity verification tools to provide a more secure, efficient and convenient means of identifying the parties to a transaction. They want to support the conveyancing sector to develop easy-to-use, modestly priced remote and digitally secure options for conveyancers to use with their clients. HMLR has developed a set of requirements aimed at encouraging digital identity checks.

HMLR has set a standard, known as the 'Safe Harbour Standard' which is an enhanced level of identity checking defined by reference to a set of requirements. This standard is founded on the principles within the government's Good Practice Guide 45 and involves biometric and cryptographic checking of identity and verification.

HMLR's objectives for the standard are as follows:

1. *Set out a clearly defined category of digital identity checking means that we believe are both achievable and viable with current technology and which offer the most security.*

2. *Be clear that this is not a compulsory standard. Other means of identifying parties to a transaction may still be used.*

3. *Demonstrate our confidence in the use of digital identity checks by stating that if the standard is met there will be no question that the conveyancer has done enough to identify their clients and that accordingly there is no longer any risk of HM Land Registry seeking recourse for negligence in identity checking.*

The initial consultation has closed and on 12 March 2021, HMLR published its standard. The background and discussion are in the HMLR blog and the standard is contained in PG81. The guide sets out the steps required to meet HMLR's enhanced level of digital identity verification. HMLR states that:

> *'The standard when followed, constitutes what is regarded by HM Land Registry as a discharge of the duty to verify the identity of a party to a registrable transaction.*
>
> *A conveyancer who adopts this approach will have fulfilled their obligation to take reasonable steps in relation to the requirement to verify their client's identity and will reach the "Safe Harbour". This means that if a conveyancer carries out the steps described in the standard, HM Land Registry will not pursue any recourse claim against the conveyancer resulting from the registration of a fraudulent transaction on the grounds that identity checks were inadequate.'*

Conveyancers should note that the guidance:

- sets out an alternative method / standard for checking identity and firms can use it immediately
- is separate to HMLR's requirements as to how identification evidence is to be provided in the context of an HMLR application (see PG67)
- does not deal with identity checks required by regulatory or representative bodies
- does not deal with identity checks required by law, for example, under the money laundering legislation

- is not mandatory

HMLR does not expect immediate adoption of digital identity verification tools and accepts it will be an incremental approach. HMLR is looking into how it might provide a list of certified identity check providers.

As with many of these initiatives, conveyancers (and their indemnity insurers) are only likely to be wholly supportive if all parties within the conveyancing process accept the scheme – including lenders, all conveyancers and HMRC. Conveyancers will no doubt take heart from the statement that HMLR *'must satisfy itself that there has indeed been fraud or negligence before seeking recourse against a conveyancer'*. But, as ever, the devil will be in the detail. Conveyancers and their indemnity insurers will no doubt be watching developments with interest.

Consultations

HMLR will continue to consult regarding the development of the electronic witnessed signature process and the more comprehensive qualified electronic signatures. Conveyancers are urged to respond to these consultations to ensure that their comments are received and voice is heard. The consultation responses are not publicly available.

Conveyancers are reminded that the significant announcement by HMLR on 27 July 2020 that 'witnessed' electronic signatures would be an acceptable form of signing a deed was released via the HMLR blog. It is therefore safe to assume that this will be the general method of communication with the profession moving forward.

It is almost certainly the case that HMLR will continue to refine and change their 'requirements' set out in PG82 thus conveyancers should subscribe to the blog and email updates to ensure that they stay up to date.

It would also be prudent to check the requirements in PG82 each time a conveyancer is faced with dealing with a conveyancer-certified electronic signature. Conveyancers should ensure that they are complying with the most up-to-date version of PG82 when they adopt the procedure. Conveyancers may wish to download a dated copy of PG82 and store it with their client file in case it is ever necessary to prove the applicable procedure on any given date. HMLR has suggested that it will make archived, dated copies of their requirements available for this very purpose but conveyancers may wish to take the matter into their own hands from a risk management point of view.

Government's Trust Framework

In February 2021 the Department for Digital, Culture, Media & Sport launched a consultation on a policy paper entitled 'The UK Digital Identity and Attributes Trust Framework'. The premise is that individuals should have a 'digital identity' and the aim is to build a 'trusted digital identity system for the UK'. It could be used to facilitate conveyancing. The government states that it is working on a number of issues including limitations on liability. This will no doubt be closely watched by conveyancers.

In conclusion…

Despite the fact that there are many acts which, legally, can constitute a signature, what conveyancers require, above all else, is certainty:

- They need to be as certain as possible that their own client has signed a particular document

- They need to be as certain as possible that the client of the conveyancer on the other side of the transaction is the signatory of a particular document

- They need to be certain that the contracting parties have read and understood the contents of the document which they are signing and accept the signed version as the final, agreed version

- They need to be certain that the witnessing requirements have been met

The reason that this is so vital for conveyancers is because it is often the conveyancer and their indemnity insurer in the firing line in the event that something goes wrong.

Whilst the use of electronic signatures is an important innovation, it is equally important for conveyancers to ensure that they do not let their guard down and that they properly assess the risk both across their practice if they decide to adopt electronic signatures and, on a micro level, on a file-by-file basis if a document is presented to them that is not signed using a wet signature.

It is likely that a reasonable amount of time will be required to:

- carry out the required risk reviews internally
- conduct appropriate market research to establish what is available
- implement a system
- train staff to use it properly

Conveyancing firms will need to decide whether they have an appetite for embracing conveyancer-certified electronic signatures. Many within the prop tech industry would argue that the use of an electronic signature platform reduces the risk of fraud. This is a risk assessment which each firm will need to make based on a detailed consideration of its:

- client base – firms which act for clients who are less likely to embrace or have access to technology may decide that the cost does not outweigh the benefit of acquiring new systems; fundamental to the adoption of conveyancer-certified electronic signatures is access to electronic platforms by the clients
- current methods of work – any electronic signature platform must be absorbed into the firm's current methods of working. Firms may wish to discuss with platform providers the ease with which a platform can be integrated into any existing case management system
- conveyancing staff – some staff may be more resistant to change. Firms will also need to consider the current location of their conveyancing staff and workload. It might be more challenging

for a firm to adequately train staff who are working remotely, irrespective of how IT savvy or otherwise those staff might be

- IT support/infrastructure – those firms which have an in-house IT function may feel more comfortable in subscribing to an electronic signature platform as the firm should have more control over how the platform is acquired and integrated into existing systems

- ability to train staff – central to virtually everything mentioned in this Practical Guide is the need for firms to properly train their conveyancing staff to ensure that an electronic signature platform can be implemented and used properly. This is particularly important for those conveyancers who will be required to give the appropriate certificate to HMLR regarding compliance with PG82 when submitting an application for registration.

Introducing the conveyancer-certified electronic signatures procedures into the conveyancing process will be seen as a natural progression for some firms but a seismic change for others. It is likely that those organisations which have already integrated the use of IT, case management systems and/or a conveyancing process app into their way of working will be able to source a suitable platform and integrate it relatively easily. However, the conveyancing landscape is very dispersed with a large number of organisations spread around the country. The speed with which conveyancer-certified electronic signatures become the norm, if ever, will depend on the number of firms willing to adopt the process. Remember that the first hurdle to using the process is that both conveyancers agree at the outset to do so. If one firm is unwilling to do so, the process cannot work.

The use of conveyancer-certified electronic signatures also requires a significant amount of collaboration between the conveyancers acting for the seller and buyer. This Practical Guide makes a number of suggestions, which are not part of HMLR's specified requirements that could provide extra protection for the buyer's conveyancer. They are likely to want information about the platform used by the seller's conveyancer, the security procedures, the process, data storage, to enable them to assess the level of risk that they might be taking on when giving the certificate at the time they make their HMLR application. If the attitude of the seller's conveyancer is to refuse such requests, it is likely that many conveyancers acting for the buyer will not be prepared to take the risk.

Whether a conveyancing firm is prepared to expend the time and money required to use conveyancer-certified electronic signatures is a decision for each firm. They will each have different client bases, staff competencies, systems and attitudes to risk. All of these factors will determine whether a conveyancing firm is going to seek out a platform provider and embrace conveyancer-certified electronic signatures.

APPENDIX

RESOURCES

Throughout this Practical Guide, conveyancers are referred to source material for further detail or guidance. The law and practice in relation to electronic signatures is fast moving and, in particular, HMLR is regularly reviewing its procedures. Accordingly, practitioners should ensure that they refer to the latest copy of any HMLR Practice Guide or document referred to.

The key source material is listed below and, where quoted, copyright is fully acknowledged.

HMLR website and Practice Guides

https://www.gov.uk/government/organisations/land-registry

Practice guide 8: Execution of deeds (PG8)

Practice Guide 9: Powers of attorney and registered land (PG9)

Practice Guide 19: Notices, restrictions and protection of third-party interests (PG19)

Practice guide 31: Discharge of charges (PG31)

Practice Guide 39: Rectification and indemnity (PG39)

Practice Guide 67: Evidence of identity: conveyancers (PG67)

Practice Guide 68: Amending deeds that effect dispositions of registered land (PG68)

Practice Guide 73: Statements of truth (PG73)

Practice Guide 81: Encouraging the use of digital technology in identity verification (PG81)

Practice Guide 82: Electronic signatures accepted by HM Land Registry (PG82)

https://www.gov.uk/government/publications/electronic-signatures-accepted-by-hm-land-registry-pg82/practice-guide-82-electronic-signatures-accepted-by-hm-land-registry#appendix-1

HM Land Registry: digital applications

https://www.gov.uk/guidance/hm-land-registry-digital-applications

HMLR: Sign your mortgage deed

https://www.gov.uk/government/publications/hm-land-registry-sign-your-mortgage-deed

HMLR blog

https://hmlandregistry.blog.gov.uk/

Law Society Practice Guides

www.lawsociety.org.uk

The Law Society has issued the following practice notes in response to case law and HMLR changes in this area:

Execution of documents by virtual means (16.02.2010)

https://www.lawsociety.org.uk/topics/business-management/execution-of-documents-by-virtual-means

Execution of a document using an electronic signature (21.07.2019)

https://www.lawsociety.org.uk/topics/business-management/execution-of-a-document-using-and-electronic-signature

Both of the above were updated by the Law Society (18.06.2020) as a result of the Covid-19 situation which brought an urgency to the requirement for conveyancers to be able to use electronic signatures https://www.lawsociety.org.uk/topics/coronavirus/our-position-on-the-use-of-virtual-execution-and-e-signature-during-the-coronavirus-covid19-pandemic

Other Law Society Resources

Law Society's Formulae for Exchanging Contracts by Telephone

https://www.lawsociety.org.uk/en/topics/property/formulae-for-exchanging-contracts-by-telephone

The Law Society Code for Completion by Post (2019)

https://www.lawsociety.org.uk/en/topics/property/code-for-completion-by-post

Law Commission

'Electronic execution of documents', Law Commission (2019) (Law Com No 386)

https://www.lawcom.gov.uk/project/electronic-execution-of-documents/

Working Group

Electronic Execution of Documents: Industry Working Group Interim Report (01.02.2022)

https://assets.publishing.service.gov.uk/government/uploads/system/uploads/attachment_data/file/1051451/electronic-execution-documents-industry-working-group-interim-report.pdf

Note that consultation on this Report are on going; practitioners interested In this area should subscribe to relevant updates.

ICO website

www.ico.org.uk

Legal Sector Affinity Group Guidance Anti-Money Laundering Guidance for the Legal Sector 2021 (LSAG Guidance)

https://www.sra.org.uk/globalassets/documents/solicitors/firm-based-authorisation/lsag-aml-guidance.pdf?version=49d62e

MORE BOOKS BY LAW BRIEF PUBLISHING

A selection of our other titles available now:-

'A Practical Guide to Parental Alienation in Private and Public Law Children Cases' by Sam King QC & Frankie Shama
'Contested Heritage – Removing Art from Land and Historic Buildings' by Richard Harwood QC, Catherine Dobson, David Sawtell
'The Limits of Separate Legal Personality: When Those Running a Company Can Be Held Personally Liable for Losses Caused to Third Parties Outside of the Company' by Dr Mike Wilkinson
'A Practical Guide to Transgender Law' by Robin Moira White & Nicola Newbegin
'Artificial Intelligence – The Practical Legal Issues (2nd Edition)' by John Buyers
'A Practical Guide to Residential Freehold Conveyancing' by Lorraine Richardson
'A Practical Guide to Pensions on Divorce for Lawyers' by Bryan Scant
'A Practical Guide to Challenging Sham Marriage Allegations in Immigration Law' by Priya Solanki
'A Practical Guide to Legal Rights in Scotland' by Sarah-Jane Macdonald
'A Practical Guide to New Build Conveyancing' by Paul Sams & Rebecca East
'A Practical Guide to Defending Barristers in Disciplinary Cases' by Marc Beaumont
'A Practical Guide to Inherited Wealth on Divorce' by Hayley Trim
'A Practical Guide to Practice Direction 12J and Domestic Abuse in Private Law Children Proceedings' by Rebecca Cross & Malvika Jaganmohan
'A Practical Guide to Confiscation and Restraint' by Narita Bahra QC, John Carl Townsend, David Winch
'A Practical Guide to the Law of Forests in Scotland' by Philip Buchan
'A Practical Guide to Health and Medical Cases in Immigration Law' by Rebecca Chapman & Miranda Butler
'A Practical Guide to Bad Character Evidence for Criminal Practitioners by Aparna Rao
'A Practical Guide to Extradition Law post-Brexit' by Myles Grandison et al

'A Practical Guide to Hoarding and Mental Health for Housing Lawyers' by Rachel Coyle
'A Practical Guide to Psychiatric Claims in Personal Injury – 2nd Edition' by Liam Ryan
'Stephens on Contractual Indemnities' by Richard Stephens
'A Practical Guide to the EU Succession Regulation' by Richard Frimston
'A Practical Guide to Solicitor and Client Costs – 2nd Edition' by Robin Dunne
'Constructive Dismissal – Practice Pointers and Principles' by Benjimin Burgher
'A Practical Guide to Religion and Belief Discrimination Claims in the Workplace' by Kashif Ali
'A Practical Guide to the Law of Medical Treatment Decisions' by Ben Troke
'Fundamental Dishonesty and QOCS in Personal Injury Proceedings: Law and Practice' by Jake Rowley
'A Practical Guide to the Law in Relation to School Exclusions' by Charlotte Hadfield & Alice de Coverley
'A Practical Guide to Divorce for the Silver Separators' by Karin Walker
'The Right to be Forgotten – The Law and Practical Issues' by Melissa Stock
'A Practical Guide to Planning Law and Rights of Way in National Parks, the Broads and AONBs' by James Maurici QC, James Neill et al
'A Practical Guide to Election Law' by Tom Tabori
'A Practical Guide to the Law in Relation to Surrogacy' by Andrew Powell
'A Practical Guide to Claims Arising from Fatal Accidents – 2nd Edition' by James Patience
'A Practical Guide to the Ownership of Employee Inventions – From Entitlement to Compensation' by James Tumbridge & Ashley Roughton
'A Practical Guide to Asbestos Claims' by Jonathan Owen & Gareth McAloon
'A Practical Guide to Stamp Duty Land Tax in England and Northern Ireland' by Suzanne O'Hara
'A Practical Guide to the Law of Farming Partnerships' by Philip Whitcomb
'Covid-19, Homeworking and the Law – The Essential Guide to Employment and GDPR Issues' by Forbes Solicitors
'Covid-19 and Criminal Law – The Essential Guide' by Ramya Nagesh
'Covid-19 and Family Law in England and Wales – The Essential Guide' by Safda Mahmood

'A Practical Guide to the Law of Unlawful Eviction and Harassment – 2nd Edition' by Stephanie Lovegrove
'Covid-19, Brexit and the Law of Commercial Leases – The Essential Guide' by Mark Shelton
'A Practical Guide to Costs in Personal Injury Claims – 2nd Edition' by Matthew Hoe
'A Practical Guide to the General Data Protection Regulation (GDPR) – 2nd Edition' by Keith Markham
'Ellis on Credit Hire – Sixth Edition' by Aidan Ellis & Tim Kevan
'A Practical Guide to Working with Litigants in Person and McKenzie Friends in Family Cases' by Stuart Barlow
'Protecting Unregistered Brands: A Practical Guide to the Law of Passing Off' by Lorna Brazell
'A Practical Guide to Secondary Liability and Joint Enterprise Post-Jogee' by Joanne Cecil & James Mehigan
'A Practical Guide to the Pre-Action RTA Claims Protocol for Personal Injury Lawyers' by Antonia Ford
'A Practical Guide to Neighbour Disputes and the Law' by Alexander Walsh
'A Practical Guide to Forfeiture of Leases' by Mark Shelton
'A Practical Guide to Coercive Control for Legal Practitioners and Victims' by Rachel Horman
'A Practical Guide to Rights Over Airspace and Subsoil' by Daniel Gatty
'Tackling Disclosure in the Criminal Courts – A Practitioner's Guide' by Narita Bahra QC & Don Ramble
'A Practical Guide to the Law of Driverless Cars – Second Edition' by Alex Glassbrook, Emma Northey & Scarlett Milligan
'A Practical Guide to TOLATA Claims' by Greg Williams
'A Practical Guide to Elderly Law – 2nd Edition' by Justin Patten
'A Practical Guide to Responding to Housing Disrepair and Unfitness Claims' by Iain Wightwick
'A Practical Guide to the Construction and Rectification of Wills and Trust Instruments' by Edward Hewitt
'A Practical Guide to the Law of Bullying and Harassment in the Workplace' by Philip Hyland
'How to Be a Freelance Solicitor: A Practical Guide to the SRA-Regulated Freelance Solicitor Model' by Paul Bennett

'A Practical Guide to Prison Injury Claims' by Malcolm Johnson
'A Practical Guide to the Small Claims Track - 2nd Edition' by Dominic Bright
'A Practical Guide to Advising Clients at the Police Station' by Colin Stephen McKeown-Beaumont
'A Practical Guide to Antisocial Behaviour Injunctions' by Iain Wightwick
'Practical Mediation: A Guide for Mediators, Advocates, Advisers, Lawyers, and Students in Civil, Commercial, Business, Property, Workplace, and Employment Cases' by Jonathan Dingle with John Sephton
'The Mini-Pupillage Workbook' by David Boyle
'A Practical Guide to Crofting Law' by Brian Inkster
'A Practical Guide to Spousal Maintenance' by Liz Cowell
'A Practical Guide to the Law of Domain Names and Cybersquatting' by Andrew Clemson
'A Practical Guide to the Law of Gender Pay Gap Reporting' by Harini Iyengar
'A Practical Guide to the Rights of Grandparents in Children Proceedings' by Stuart Barlow
'NHS Whistleblowing and the Law' by Joseph England
'Employment Law and the Gig Economy' by Nigel Mackay & Annie Powell
'A Practical Guide to Noise Induced Hearing Loss (NIHL) Claims' by Andrew Mckie, Ian Skeate, Gareth McAloon
'An Introduction to Beauty Negligence Claims – A Practical Guide for the Personal Injury Practitioner' by Greg Almond
'Intercompany Agreements for Transfer Pricing Compliance' by Paul Sutton
'Zen and the Art of Mediation' by Martin Plowman
'A Practical Guide to the SRA Principles, Individual and Law Firm Codes of Conduct 2019 – What Every Law Firm Needs to Know' by Paul Bennett
'A Practical Guide to Adoption for Family Lawyers' by Graham Pegg
'A Practical Guide to Industrial Disease Claims' by Andrew Mckie & Ian Skeate
'A Practical Guide to Redundancy' by Philip Hyland
'A Practical Guide to Vicarious Liability' by Mariel Irvine
'A Practical Guide to Applications for Landlord's Consent and Variation of Leases' by Mark Shelton
'A Practical Guide to Relief from Sanctions Post-Mitchell and Denton' by Peter Causton

www.ingramcontent.com/pod-product-compliance
Ingram Content Group UK Ltd.
Pitfield, Milton Keynes, MK11 3LW, UK
UKHW020146290926
15471UKWH00004B/714

9 781914 608575